OREGON ROCK
A CLIMBER'S GUIDE

Jeff Thomas

The Mountaineers/Seattle

Published by The Mountaineers
715 Pike Street, Seattle, Washington 98101

Manufactured in the United States of America
Cover photos by Alan Kearney. Bill Ramsey leading Karate Crack, Smith Rock.
Book design by Marge Mueller
Cover design by Elizabeth Watson
Map by Claire Shelton

Library of Congress Cataloging in Publication Data

Thomas, Jeff (Jeffrey Paxton)
  Oregon rock.

  Includes index.
  1. Rock climbing—Oregon—Guide-books. 2. Oregon—Description
and travel—1951- —Guide-books. I. Title.
GV199.42.O7T56 1983   917.95   82-18836
ISBN 0-89886-040-7 (pbk.)

Opposite, Alan Watts on the third pitch of Monkey Space, Smith Rock

(Chris Jones photo)

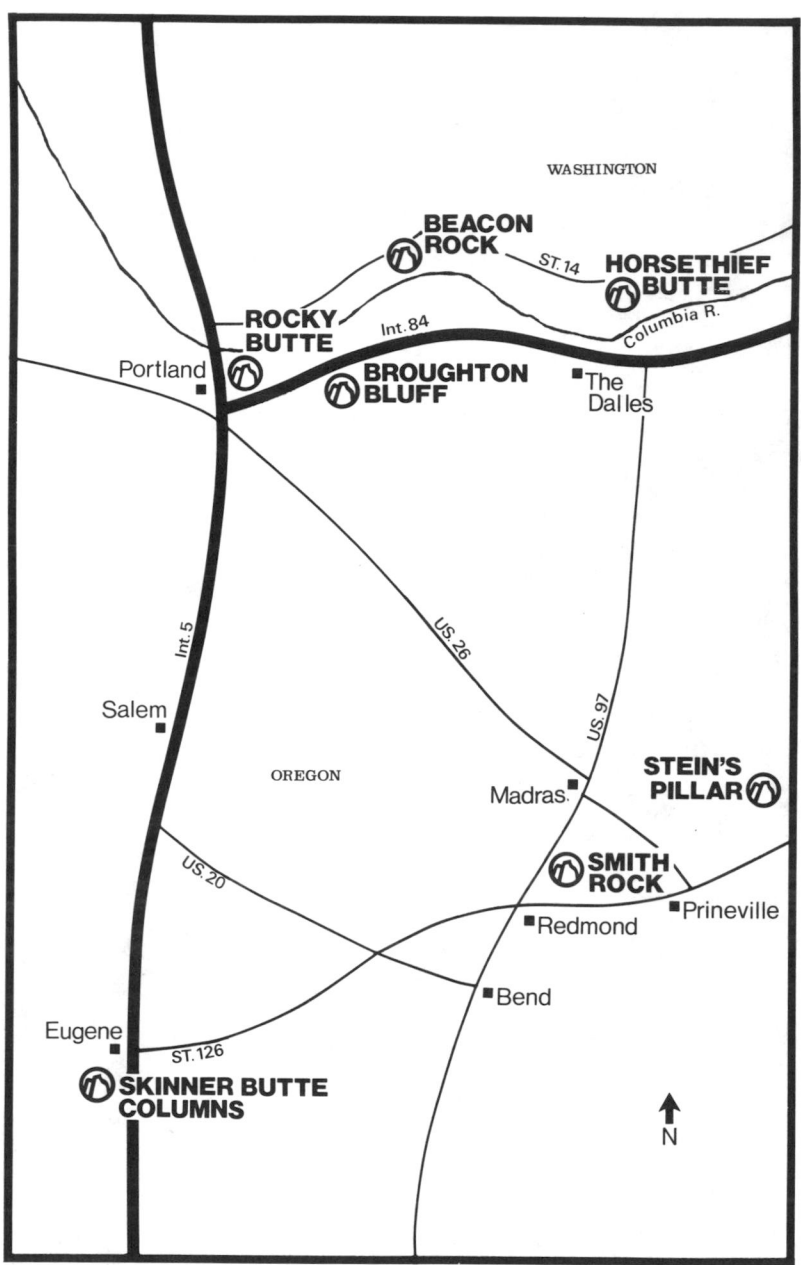

TABLE OF CONTENTS

INTRODUCTION

Oregon Rock is a guide to the major lowland rock climbing areas in northwestern Oregon: Broughton Bluff, Beacon Rock, Smith Rock, and Stein's Pillar (see map, page 4). In addition, three practice cliffs which are important for training and developing new skills are mentioned in the first chapter. Several areas suitable for exploratory climbing have been deliberately exluded because the purpose of this book is to record major climbing centers for those who need a guidebook.

It is assumed that the reader has some knowledge of rope management and the art of placing protection. If not, he or she should seek this advice elsewhere, preferably from competent climbers.

RATINGS

Rock climbs are rated according to difficulty. Several systems exist but the one most commonly used in Oregon, and therefore in this book, is the Yosemite Decimal System. This system is composed of three subdivisions: overall difficulty, free climbing difficulty and aid difficulty.

OVERALL DIFFICULTY

Roman numerals I through VI denote how long a climb takes for an average party.

- I   Two hours or less
- II Half day or less
- III Full day
- IV A bivouac might be needed unless the party is fast
- V   Two days
- VI Three days or longer

Most of the climbs within this book fall between grades I and III.

FREE CLIMBING DIFFICULTY

Numbers 1 through 5 are used to classify the general type of terrain a climber must pass over.

- 1 Trail hiking
- 2 Scrambling over talus or through brush
- 3 Steep slopes or exposed ridges
- 4 Steep rock requiring a rope
- 5 Rope and protection required

Class 5 is further broken down to measure the single most difficult free move on a roped climb. A decimal point and the numbers 1 through 13 are used. For example, a 5.1 climb is relatively easy and most people can climb it, while a 5.13 climb is extremely difficult and few climbers ascend it successfully. If a pitch contains a series of moves of the same difficulty, a higher number is assigned. In addition, the

Opposite, Jeff Thomas on Northeast Face, Stein's Pillar (Ken Currens photo)

system is open-ended; if a climb is done which seems more difficult than anything previously encountered, it is assigned a higher number.

A vagary exists in classes 5.10, 5.11, and 5.12. The letters A through D are used to distinguish easier climbs from more difficult climbs within each respective class. For example, a 5.10A is much easier than a 5.10D. The A through D subdivision is cumbersome, but most contemporary climbers are unfamiliar with other methods of rating free climbs. For this reason, the A through D system is used in this book.

AID DIFFICULTY

The numbers 0 through 5 following the letter A indicate aid difficulty.

A0 Pendulum, shoulder stand, tension rest or a quick move up by pulling on protection

A1 Solid placements

A2 Strenuous placements or hard-to-judge positions with solid protection

A3 Several marginal placements but nothing continuous

A4 Large number of marginal placements

A5 Protection is marginal on the entire pitch, and a long fall will result if a mistake is made.

The letter C replaces the letter A in the rating when a climb has been done without hammering pitons.

CLIMBING EQUIPMENT

Geologically, Oregon cliffs are volcanic. Volcanic rock is characteristically soft and will not withstand punishment without leaving permanent scars. Nuts, Friends, and other clean protection provide the safety of pitons and bolts without destroying the rock. In the following ways, this book strongly advocates the use of clean protection:

1. Cracks which are badly scarred and in danger of destruction are identified. If you can't do these climbs cleanly, back off and try another time.

2. Climbs which can be done cleanly are marked "nuts" with a maximum size given, if known. Do not limit your rack to nuts, however, as Friends are very useful in Oregon.

3. Where aid has been eliminated on a climb, the aid rating has been dropped and a free rating is given to encourage other free ascents.

4. Fixed pins are encouraged on certain routes where adequate protection is otherwise unavailable.

5. Placing bolts is discouraged and is not required for any of the climbs in this book.

Chalk has become very popular. Some maintain it is absolutely necessary, some that it is a permanent blemish. Both parties are correct to some degree. Restraint in the use of chalk seems to be the only answer.

Opposite, on Dod's Jam, Beacon Rock (Mark Cartier photo)

The standard rope length for the climbs in this book is 150′. Exceptions are noted in individual route descriptions.

KEY TO PHOTOGRAPHS

1. Directions always assume the climber is facing the cliff.
2. A series of line dashes indicates a main route; alternating dots and dashes indicate a variation; dots indicate that a section of the route cannot be seen from the camera's perspective.
3. Numbers correspond to numbers in the accompanying text. If a climb is not shown in the photograph, it is labeled "not shown" in the text.
4. Rappel points are indicated by a circle.
5. A number with an arrow indicates that a particular climb is just off the photo or cannot be seen from the camera's viewpoint.

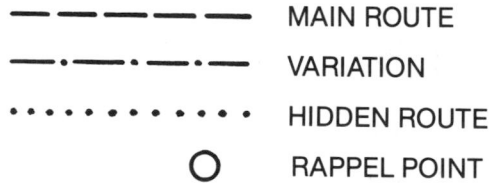

— — — — — MAIN ROUTE

—·—·—·— VARIATION

· · · · · · · · · · · HIDDEN ROUTE

○ RAPPEL POINT

1 PRACTICE AREAS

Competent climbing takes practice whether you are just starting or struggling to keep in shape on a weekday. Short cliffs or bouldering areas are ideal because one can test his or her skill on top rope without undue risk. Rocky Butte, Horsethief Butte and Skinner Butte Columns are traditional practice areas. Rocky Butte and Skinner Butte have the advantage of being located within 2 major metropolitan areas, Portland and Eugene–Springfield respectively.

Rocky Butte

Rocky Butte is a prominent landmark on the eastern boundary of northeast Portland. Climbing can be found in an abandoned rock quarry on the northeast flank of the Butte and on an artificial rock wall on top of the Butte.

TOP OF ROCKY BUTTE

The structure on top of Rocky Butte, as well as the road and tunnel that lead up to it, were constructed by the WPA in the 1930s. The rock came from a small quarry on the east side of Rocky Butte. That quarry is now covered by I-205. Over the years the structure has been used as an observation post and more recently for bouldering. The west wall of the structure is the best side to climb on.

To reach the top of Rocky Butte, take I-84 and exit onto 82nd Avenue. Turn right (north) at the T intersection and follow 82nd over the freeway. Turn right on Halsey St. and continue ½ mile to 92nd Avenue. Turn left and follow 92nd to a Y intersection. Follow the right-hand road up the hill and park in the circular drive on top.

Some may feel the need for a rope on the 15' west wall, but rock shoes are generally the only equipment necessary.

ROCKY BUTTE QUARRY

As the many blasting holes indicate, the cliff was once a privately owned quarry. It is now under the jurisdiction of the Oregon Department of Transportation and no longer operating. If one overlooks the noise from I-205 and the debris, dynamite crack climbing can be found.

The quarry is reached by taking I-84 to 82nd Avenue. At the T intersection, turn right (north) on 82nd and follow it for a mile to N.E. Fremont St. Turn right (east) on Fremont and follow the road as it curves north and changes to N.E. 91st. Immediately after 91st turns east, and just before tennis courts on the right, park in either of 2 pull-outs on the right and left sides of the road.

Aerial view of Horsethief Butte from the northwest (Don Lowe photo)

From the first pull-out, cross the street and follow a path 15′ to the cliff. Just to the left of where the path enters a clearing, there's an easy (5.1) downclimb or rappel.* At the bottom of the descent and 20′ right is a small amphitheater with several excellent crack climbs.

A second path starts at the other pull-out immediately next to a guardrail on the north side of the road. Walk to the cliff edge, then move right about 20′ to a small gully. Rappel or downclimb the gully (5.1). Moving right at the bottom, one sees several excellent crack climbs within a distance of about 60′. Exploration will yield other lines in other directions.

A top rope is generally used for climbing in the quarry. It takes some time to locate the best anchors.

Horsethief Butte

Horsethief Butte is a basaltic rock mesa with several cunningly disguised corridors leading into its interior. Along the sides of these

---

*Instructions are given as if the climber were facing the cliff.

corridors are a variety of top-rope and boulder problems. Leading is possible, but the maximum height of the walls is 30' to 40'.

Take I-84 to Exit 87 just east of The Dalles. Cross the bridge over the Columbia River and drive about 3 miles north to State 14. Turn right (east) and drive 2½ miles, passing Horsethief Lake State Park. There are 2 places to park. The first turnout is on the right by a historical marker. The second, closer turnout is on the left beyond a small bridge. A trail leads south from the second pull-out to what appears to be a blank wall. Closer inspection reveals a hidden entrance, which leads to a small amphitheater. There are numerous short climbs and boulders in this amphitheater as well as in the major canyon to the east.

Overnight camping is not allowed in or around the climbing area, but developed fee sites may be found at Horsethief Lake State Park. Undeveloped free sites can be found at Hesse or Spearfish campgrounds along the road between State 14 and the bridge.

Skinner Butte Columns

Skinner Butte Columns, known locally as the Columns, has perhaps the highest concentration of difficult top-rope climbs in the Northwest. Because of its small size and central location, climbers have explored every imaginable route and developed the art of finger crack and face climbing to a high level. An explanation of the routes and grading system is beyond the scope of this guide. Further information is available in a small, out-of-print guide. Reference copies are kept at the River House, 301 North Adams Street, Eugene, and at the Outdoor Program, Eugene Parks and Recreation Department.

To reach Skinner Butte Columns, exit I-5 onto I-105. Follow I-105 to its end at 7th Avenue. Follow 7th Avenue east 3 blocks and turn left (north) on Lincoln. Approximately 6 blocks later, Lincoln tops a small rise on the west side of Skinner Butte. On the right side of the intersection is a parking lot and the Columns.

2 BROUGHTON BLUFF

Broughton Bluff is a general name for a series of cliffs overlooking the eastern shore of the Sandy River. There are 10 separate cliffs. This book details those 6 with public access from Lewis and Clark State Park. From north to south these include the North Face, Hanging Gardens Wall, Red Wall, Bridge Cliff, Trident, and Bat Wall.

The Bluff was created by a lava flow from nearby Chamberlain Hill. The flow apparently did not have sufficient time to cool, as columnar jointing is not complete and the cliffs are amorphous, chaotic, and well-vegetated. For the climber this means dirty rock, difficult route finding, fewer cracks, and several routes where fixed pins are necessary. Fixed pins are standard on some Broughton Bluff climbs. Please respect the next party and leave them in place.

Poison oak and nettles are also a problem, although general use has beaten them back in the more popular areas. Outweighing the geologic and botanical drawbacks are easy access (less than 20 miles or 25 minutes from downtown Portland), and southwest orientation (which provides comfortable temperatures in winter and blocks the ferocious Columbia Gorge winds).

To reach the cliffs, take Exit 18 off I-84 for Lewis and Clark State Park. Turn left at the T intersection, go under the railroad tracks and park in a state park day-use area under the North Face. Walk south along the highway to the steep hillside below the North Face and follow the path that begins near the road. The path forks where it meets rock; take the left fork to reach the North Face, and follow the right path to reach the remaining cliffs. The descent line for the North Face and Hanging Gardens Wall is down third class ledges just to the left of the spot where the path forks.

North Face

From the fork in the trail, contour left approximately 200'. The trail ends below the obvious cliff face seen from the state park parking lot.

1 GANDALF'S GRIP
II, 5.9; nuts to 3"

Start in the middle of the cliff in an alcove with broken rock. *First Pitch:* Climb 8' to good rock and the start of a thin crack. Follow the crack about 30' and traverse left on face holds to a right-facing dihedral. Belay above on a detached flake. *Second Pitch:* Climb a right-leaning ramp until holds disappear, and force a mantle over the overhang (known as Gollum's Hang) above. Traverse left 15' and belay. *Third*

Pitch: Follow the obvious dihedral above to a ledge. *Fourth Pitch:* Thrash up a short off-size crack to the top.

2 *Variation I:* LEANING PILLAR
5.10A or B

Reach the first belay by climbing a right-facing dihedral 10' to the left of the regular start. The crux is gaining the dihedral, which is reached either by clawing up directly from below (5.10B) or moving subtly in from higher on the left (5.10A).

3 *Variation II*
5.6

Start 15' left of Gandalf's and climb loose rock and mossy cracks to the first belay. Continue up Gandalf's Grip or traverse left under an overhang to a pillar. Surmount the overhang using the pillar and traverse right to rejoin Gandalf's at the second belay.

4 PEACH CLING
II, 5.11-AO; nuts to 2", mostly small wires

The crux is highlighted by a large flake that you must use for both climbing and protection, although it does not feel as if it will hold your weight. Start as for Gandalf's Grip. *First Pitch:* Climb a thin crack 10' to the right of the normal start for Gandalf's Grip. Where the crack ends, climb a shallow corner to a bolt belay. *Second Pitch:* Move up and left via strenuous and off-balance moves to a large belay ledge (the same belay ledge as for the third pitch of Gandalf's). *Third Pitch:* Continue left on a left-slanting ledge to the top.

Hanging Gardens Wall

The right fork of the parking lot path leads 30' around a corner to the start of Hanging Gardens Wall. The first horizontal 100' of this cliff is less than 60' high and is generally used for top-roping or bouldering. The distinguishing feature is **5 THE SICKLE** (I, 5.7 or 5.8; not shown), a curving jam crack at the very beginning of the cliff. There are other named climbs, but the uniform nature of the rock makes it difficult to differentiate among them. It is best to choose a couple of cracks, set a top rope and have at it.

One hundred feet after The Sickle, the cliff reaches about 150' in height. The bottom one-third is characterized by detached basalt columns with cracks every few feet. It is relatively easy (I, 5.5 to 5.8) to climb these columns and there is usually a good place to belay at the top. The upper two-thirds of the cliff is steep with very few cracks. Those cracks that do exist are quite difficult. The southeast end of the cliff is dirty and vegetated and is of little interest to the climber.

Opposite, North Face (Alan Kearney photo)

6 LOOSE BLOCK OVERHANG
I, 5.9; nuts to 2″

The name has stuck but the loose block fell out long ago. Follow the trail under Hanging Gardens Wall until the cliff begins to get higher. The climb starts just left of a large maple tree growing out of the cliff. *First Pitch:* Chimney and jam to the top of a semi-detached column. Jam a crack up a slightly overhung wall (crux) and continue up another 20′ to a good ledge. *Second Pitch:* Jam a left-facing corner for several feet and "swing" right to a slab. Move right 5′ and climb a blocky overhang to the top.

7 LEAST RESISTANCE
I, 5.10A; nuts to 2″, fixed pins

A one-move climb. Start as for Hanging Gardens. *First Pitch:* Climb to the maple tree on Hanging Gardens. *Second Pitch:* Traverse left 15′. Step up to a seam and follow it left around a corner (crux). Climb up to a good belay. *Third Pitch:* Follow the last pitch of Loose Block Overhang.

8 SANDY'S DIRECT
I, 5.10C; nuts to 1″, fixed pins

A good climb if the fixed pins are still there. Start as for Hanging Gardens. *First Pitch:* Climb to the maple tree on Hanging Gardens. *Second Pitch:* Climb up and slightly left to a corner with a fixed pin. Climb over a slight bulge and follow a corner, passing another bulge on the way to the top.

9 FACE NOT FRICTION
I, 5.11D; nuts to ½″

A puzzling name for an equally puzzling climb. *First Pitch:* Climb to the maple tree on Hanging Gardens. *Second Pitch:* Climb up to the base of an overhanging face. Rise past 2 bolts and over a small roof (crux). Climb a thin crack above to the top.

10 HANGING GARDENS
II, 5.10A or 5.6-A1; nuts to 1½″, fixed pins

The crux is a refreshing change from the norm; that is, you don't have to undergo excruxiating pain in order to do difficult climbing. Start below a small maple tree that is growing out of the cliff about 30′ off the ground. The columns on either side of the start are covered with bright yellow lichen, so you can't miss the route. *First Pitch:* It is possible to climb straight up to the maple tree, but it is much more enjoyable to climb the crack system that starts 10′ to the left. Belay at the maple.

Left half of Hanging Gardens Wall (Alan Kearney photo)

Second Pitch: Move right 10' on a slab, climb over an overhang and traverse right 30' to 40'. Climb an easy corner to a good ledge and a bolt belay. *Third Pitch:* Traverse right around a blind corner. Work free or with aid (fixed pins) horizontally right 20' on the "bicycle path" to the grassy ledges and an oak tree belay. Scramble to the top. Watch out for poison oak.

11 *Variation I:* BFD

5.9

Begin right of the regular start below a large maple tree growing out of the cliff 6' from the ground. Climb onto a large flake above the tree and make a difficult move up and left to rejoin Hanging Gardens.

12 *Variation II:* MR. POTATO

5.11A; nuts to ¾"

Begin below a large maple tree growing out of the cliff 6' from the ground. Climb up and right to a short right-facing corner below a large roof. Pull and stem over the roof and move left and up to the Hanging Gardens traverse. Rappel or climb any of the routes above.

13 *Variation III:* FUN IN THE MUD

5.10C; nuts to ¾"

Start 10' to the right of a large maple growing out of the cliff 6' from the ground. Climb 20' up the right side of a smooth slab, then move left to the base of a roof split by a thin crack. If mud is not choking the crack, follow it to the traverse on the second pitch of Hanging Gardens. Rappel or climb any of the routes above.

The next 5 climbs share the first pitch of Hanging Gardens, but branch off from the second pitch in an amphitheater above.

14 *Variation IV:* SESAME STREET

5.9; nuts to 2½"

Excellent but short hand jamming. *First Pitch:* Climb the first pitch of Hanging Gardens. *Second Pitch:* Step right 10' on a slab, climb over an overhang, and begin traversing right. When possible, climb up and left to the base of an overhanging wall with a prominent Z-shaped crack. *Third Pitch:* Climb crack and belay on a ledge above. *Fourth Pitch:* Fourth class horizontally left to the top.

15 *Variation V:* DEMIAN

5.10D; nuts to 1½"

Speed is safety on this one. *First and Second Pitches:* Climb to the base of Sesame Street. *Third Pitch:* Climb unprotected 5.8 moves

Right half of Hanging Gardens Wall (Alan Kearney photo)

directly above the belay to a right-facing, left-leaning dihedral. Follow the dihedral to the top.

16 *Variation VI:* ENDLESS SLEEP
5.11A; nuts to 2″

Unsafe at any speed. *First and Second Pitches:* Climb to the base of Sesame Street. *Third Pitch:* Move right 5′ and climb an unprotected, shallow right-facing corner. Above is an obvious overhanging wall with a large block stuck in the bottom of a thin crack. Gain top of block (crux), and follow the thin crack to the top.

17 *Variation VII:* PEER PRESSURE
5.10C; fixed pins

Poor protection. *First and Second Pitches:* Climb the first 2 pitches of Hanging Gardens. *Third Pitch:* Difficult, unprotected face climbing just above the belay leads to an overhanging corner. Follow it to the top.

18 *Variation VIII:* SCORPION SEAMS
5.9-A3; nuts and pins to 1″ (not shown)

First and Second Pitches: Climb the first 2 pitches of Hanging Gardens. *Third Pitch:* From the belay, mantle on top of a pillar to the right (unprotected). Nail up overhanging seams to a mantle at the top.

Red Wall

From the southern end of Hanging Gardens Wall, the trail follows a rotten log, then descends steeply to a small cliff called Red Wall. At the base of Red Wall is a blank vertical face split by a beautiful fissure called **19 CLASSIC CRACK** (I, 5.9). The crack ends 40′ up on a large ledge with a maple tree. This ledge can also be gained easily from the trail before it descends steeply. Rather than walk down from the top of Red Wall, it is better to rappel using 2 ropes from trees at the top of the cliff, especially if you are susceptible to poison oak.

20 PHYSICAL GRAFFITI
II, 5.10D; nuts to 2″

The crux is a beautiful hand crack. Start on the left side of Classic Crack ledge. *First Pitch:* Climb a corner for approximately 30′. Traverse right 30′ to a belay under a roof split by a hand crack. *Second Pitch:* Climb the crack to a ledge above. Traverse down and right and follow a corner to a tree. Rappel.

Opposite, lower portion of Red Wall (Alan Kearney photo)

21 *Variation I:* HIT THE HIGHWAY
5.11A

Start behind the maple on the Classic Crack belay ledge. Face climb up and right over a bulge to a two-bolt belay. Move right, then up and left. Climb an ominous corner to the base of the hand crack on Physical Graffiti.

22 *Variation II*
5.10A

Climb a poorly protected corner above the hand crack to the top.

23 RED EYE
II, 5.10C; nuts to 2½″

Begin on the right side of the Classic Crack belay ledge. *First Pitch:* Climb up to a bolt. Using potholes, reach a hidden ledge and hand traverse right. Move up and back left to a bolt belay in a dish. *Second Pitch:* Move right and up to a dihedral and chimney capped by large blocks. Climb over blocks and traverse left to a corner. Climb corner to the top. Rappel.

24 CRITICAL MASS
II, 5.11A; fixed pins and bolts

First Pitch: Climb the first 30′ of Sheer Stress. Continue up an overhanging groove past fixed protection to a large ceiling. Mantle and face climb past 2 bolts to the upper dihedral on Red Eye. *Second Pitch:* Finish up the last section of Red Eye.

25 SHEER STRESS
II, 5.10A; nuts to 2½″

Begin to the right of Classic Crack below a left-facing dihedral. *First Pitch:* Face climb to dihedral. Follow dihedral to a roof. Exit right and traverse 20′. Belay in a semi-hanging position on top of a block below a bulge. *Second Pitch:* Reach over to a left-facing corner and follow it to the top. Exit right.

26 *Variation*
5.10C

After exiting right on the first pitch, climb over a bulge above and traverse up and left to Red Eye. Poorly protected.

Upper portion of Red Wall and Bridge Cliff (Alan Kearney photo)

27 JOURNEY TO THE CENTER OF THE BRAIN

I, 5.9 (not shown)

Climb a detached column (the spinal column) which is 20′ to the right of Sheer Stress. Gain an alcove above (the cerebral folds). Rappel from poor anchors. Not recommended.

Bridge Cliff

The climbs on Bridge Cliff are short but the protection, rock, and climbing are excellent. Take 2 ropes for rappelling off the top.

To reach the cliff, hike past the end of Red Wall 100′ to a short wall with many columns. Skirt this wall on its right side and bushwhack up to a ledge system below a larger cliff.

28 WALK ON THE WILD SIDE

II, 5.10B; nuts to 1½″

To begin, move left on the ledge system about 25′. *First Pitch:* Face climb and mantle to a small ledge. Continue up and right to a good belay. This pitch is poorly protected. *Second Pitch:* Traverse horizontally left 15′ past a central corner to a second corner leaning left. Walk on the wild side up the corner to the top. Rappel.

29 SPIDERMONKEY

II, 5.9; nuts to 2″

Move left on the ledge system about 15′ to start. *First Pitch:* Jam, face climb, and layback past 2 small overhangs to the Walk on the Wild Side belay ledge. *Second Pitch:* Move left 5′ and climb a dark dihedral to the top. Rappel.

30 FRUIT BAT

II, 5.10B; nuts to 1″

Start on the right side of the upper wall below a sloping dihedral capped by a large roof. *First Pitch:* Boulder up into the low-angle dihedral. Climb dihedral to a large roof then move left and up. Climb past a vegetated ledge to a second larger ledge. *Second Pitch:* Climb a thin finger crack which starts just to the right of Spidermonkey. Rappel.

31 *Variation*

5.9

Climb a short hand crack which begins 10′ right of the Walk on the Wild Side belay.

Trident

Fifty feet right of Red Wall is a small cliff with heavy vegetation on its upper section.

32 THE SPRING
I, 5.10A (not shown)

Follow a crack system in the center of the cliff to an overhang 40' up. Skirt the overhang on the left and bushwhack to the top. Rappel.

Bat Wall

A seldom-visited area 300' past Bridge Cliff.

33 HANGING TREE
III, 5.10D; nuts to 3", mostly small wires, 5 or 6 knifeblades, and Lost Arrows

Dirty and unprotected in some places, with fantastic climbing in others. A little work and this would be a great climb. Start on the left side of Bat Wall just to the left of the obvious leaning tree. *First Pitch:* Climb a short overhanging crack to a sloping ledge. Move up and left until holds lead up and back right past 2 fixed pins to a sloping belay ledge. *Second Pitch:* Climb a painful thin crack to a roof. Traverse right past the roof and up a right-facing corner to a hanging tree belay. *Third Pitch:* Friction down a ramp 10' and around a blind corner to a 2-bolt belay. The bolts are only ¼" and should be backed up by a third ³⁄₈" bolt. *Fourth Pitch:* Difficult and poorly protected stemming leads up a corner to a good ledge. Traverse left 5' around a corner and climb a steep slab using unorthodox but substantial side pulls. Step left and climb blocks to a cramped belay in an alcove. *Fifth Pitch:* A wild but moderate traverse leads right 10' until easy face climbing up to a ledge. Continue straight up to a short crack using side pulls. Follow the crack up and left to the summit.

34 UNNAMED AID ROUTE
I, A3; knifeblades

Start just to the right of the obvious leaning tree. Follow a thin seam to a rappel bolt. Rappel.

35 SNAP, CRACKLE, POP
II, A3; thin pins and small nuts

Start at the large sharp-topped flake 30' right of the obvious leaning tree. *First Pitch:* Climb flake, aid right, then follow a shallow seam to a

Left half of Bat Wall

Right half of Bat Wall (Alan Kearney photos)

bolt. Cut right to free climbing right and up. Belay on a ledge. *Second Pitch:* Aid straight up and follow a bolt ladder over a roof. Rappel.

36 SUPERSTITION

III, 5.11A; nuts to 2″, fixed pins

With use, this climb will become one of the best routes at Broughton Bluff. Begin in the middle of Bat Wall in a groove just to the right of an old beehive and 2 false start bolts. *First Pitch:* Climb the groove past many fixed pins to an alcove. Move left around a bulge (first crux) and up to a good belay. *Second Pitch:* Climb past fixed pins to the base of a large roof (second crux), and move right and up to an alcove. Move back left and up around a corner and climb to a good ledge with a bolt. *Third Pitch:* Follow a right-arching corner to the top.

37 WELL HUNG

I, 5.10A or B; nuts to ¾″, fixed pins

Several large boulders sit at the base of the south end of Bat Wall. Above these boulders is a slot with a large wedged block forming a roof. Above the roof is a small ledge with a tree. The object is to get from the ground to the tree, so hang in there.

38 *Variation:* MYSTIC VOID

5.10A

Start at a thin crack to the left of the roof on Well Hung. Follow the thin crack to the small tree belay for Well Hung. Rappel.

39 GOLD ARCH

I, 5.11A

Start 35′ to the right of Well Hung at the base of a slab. *First Pitch:* Climb the slab up and slightly left. Boulder through a slot in a roof and climb a short, strenuous barndoor lieback on a gold-streaked wall. Belay at bolts above. *Second Pitch:* One hard face move leads to easier climbing and the top.

40 SHADOW DANCING

I, 5.9-A2 (not shown)

Begin in a left-facing dihedral on the far right side of Bat Wall. Jam, face climb, and aid up corner to a belay. Rappel.

3 BEACON ROCK

Beacon Rock is 35 miles east of Portland on the Washington side of the Columbia River. To reach the climbs, follow State 14 east from Vancouver or west from Bridge of the Gods. Park in the eastern end of the restroom parking lot immediately adjacent to State 14, and below the north side of Beacon Rock. A developed trail starts from the far eastern end of the parking lot. Follow it to the base of the river face, where the climbing begins. A guide to prominent landmarks, which appears later in this chapter, will be useful in locating the base of each route.

Beacon Rock is part of the Washington State Park system. Please observe the following park rules while climbing:

1. State law requires climbers to sign in and out. A bulletin board and climbing register have been set up at the eastern end of the restroom parking lot to simplify the procedure.
2. Climbing is limited to the river or south face because loose rock dislodged by climbers would endanger pedestrian traffic on the west side hiking trail and motorists at the north side facilities. Please respect this limitation. Any violation would seriously jeopardize the privilege of climbing on Beacon Rock.
3. The park discourages climbers from parking in the boat ramp and camping area west of Beacon Rock. The amount of space for automobiles is limited and the railroad company does not like climbers walking along its tracks.

There are 2 ever-present hazards at Beacon Rock: poison oak and rockfall. Poison oak proliferates at the rock's base and can best be avoided by wearing longer clothing and washing immediately after climbing. Rockfall is a serious problem, especially on weekends, originating primarily from above Dod's Jam where the west side hiking trail is closest to the river face. Sometimes the rockfall is accidental, but often rocks are thrown intentionally at individuals on climbs or on the ground. Two climbers have been struck by rocks here in the last five years (as of 1982), and there have been countless close calls. Consequently, the author strongly recommends use of a hard hat when approaching the rock and standing at its base.

The inexperienced should be forewarned that there are no easy routes on Beacon Rock and it is not a good place to practice. Anyone attempting even the southeast face should be experienced in leading, route finding, and retreating off of multi-pitch climbs.

Do not let the negative aspects of Beacon Rock deter you. The rock is extremely sound and protection, unless otherwise noted, will stop a charging rhino in its tracks. As the saying goes, it's the best place to climb in Oregon, even if it is in Washington.

Beacon Rock from the southwest (Don Lowe photo)

LOCATING THE CLIMBS FROM THE GROUND

Start on the right (southeast) side of the river face at the railroad tracks. Negotiate the protection fence and follow a beaten path 30' to the spot where the rock begins. As the evidence indicates, this is the roping-up spot for the popular Southeast Face and Right Gull. Continue west up a small incline to a 2'-high tunnel, which disappears into the rock. Directly above is a seam, the direct start of Bluebird. To the right of the tunnel are 4 dihedrals. From left to right, they are: 1 Left Gull, 2 an unclimbed dihedral, 3 Seagull, and 4 Wrong Gull. To the left of the tunnel is the dihedral which Sufficiently Breathless follows. About 100' to the west, the trail passes a small pedestal of basalt isolated from the main cliff. This pedestal is the start for all the climbs between Bluebird and Wild Turkeys. A little farther along, the trail passes a second tunnel which is the start of Dirty Double Overhang and Smooth Dancer. About 20' left of the tunnel is the start of Take Fist, which follows an indistinct line up dirty slabs and corners. From the second tunnel, follow the cliff to a third tunnel. Here is the start for all climbs between Flying Swallow and Dod's Jam. About 20' west of the third cave is a 15' flake. Free for All follows the crack directly above the flake and Free for Some the crack immediately to the left. Fifteen feet farther, on the right side of a shattered cave, is a long seam called Pipeline. Continue west until the trail ends. Above is an ugly ridge leading to all climbs between Updraft to Heaven and On the Move.

DESCENTS

All climbs eventually lead to the west side hiking trail. Routes west of, and including Smooth Dancer, end on this trail. Routes east of Smooth Dancer require relatively easy (5.4) climbing on what is known as Grassy Ledges, the broken area above the eastern half of the river face. To reach the hiking trail from Grassy Ledges, follow indistinct trails through a brushy section to an easy chimney. Climb up the chimney 20' to a ramp and follow it up and right about 60' to a bolt. Easy (5.4) moves lead left to another ramp system which eventually ends on the west-side trail. As an alternative, follow the first ramp to a tree at its top. Gain the ridge above and follow it to the west-side trail. The former method is not obvious, but once you have done it, it is much quicker.

Fixed rappels also exist on Dod's Jam (starting at Big Ledge), Flying Swallow, Take Fist, and at the point where Right and Left Gull meet and from Tree Ledge on the Southeast Face. Two ropes are needed for all of these rappels.

GARDENING

A staggering amount of work has gone into cleaning dirt, plants and lichen from most of the climbs at Beacon Rock. Despite these efforts, some climbs grow over each year and must be gardened if you wish to repeat them.

ROUTE DESCRIPTIONS

Most of the routes on Beacon Rock are single crack systems or are easy to follow. Rather than burden the reader with excessive description, only appropriate information such as name, grade, class, type of climbing and protection is given. It should be relatively easy to follow each route using this information, the "Locating the Climbs from the Ground" section (page 33), the photographs, and common sense. When a route is more complicated, a full route description is given.

1 OBNOXIOUS CUBBY HOLE
I, 5.7-A2; nuts to 2″

An obscure roof, split by a crack, around the corner from the Southeast Face. Not recommended.

2 SOUTHEAST FACE
III, 5.7; nuts to 2″

Most of the protection is fixed. A very good route. *First Pitch:* Climb easy ground up a small buttress on the right, then traverse left a few feet. Proceed straight up about 80′ to the left end of a large ledge with a dead snag (Snag Ledge). *Second Pitch:* Reach the base of a shattered groove by following a ledge 100′ to the right. *Third Pitch:* Climb the shattered groove up and left 20′. Move right about 15′ to a small stance on a slab. *Fourth Pitch:* Enter right-facing dihedrals which eventually force the route to the right onto the east face. Climb up to a large ledge with a tree (Tree Ledge). Three choices are now available: (a) rappel using 2 150′ ropes, (b) follow dihedrals up and left 150′ to Grassy Ledges, or (c) search for the Lost Variation.

3 *Variation I*
5.9

Before moving onto the east face, you can do a finish to Tree Ledge by fighting desperately through a notch.

4 *Variation II:* THE LOST VARIATION
5.8

This route got its name because many parties were unable to find it in the early seventies. The following route description may help. *First Pitch:* Climb 80′ toward Grassy Ledges. Traverse right (east) into a mossy bowl via a ledge system. *Second Pitch:* Climb a face split by a crack. Go right around a corner and follow a horizontal ledge to the east

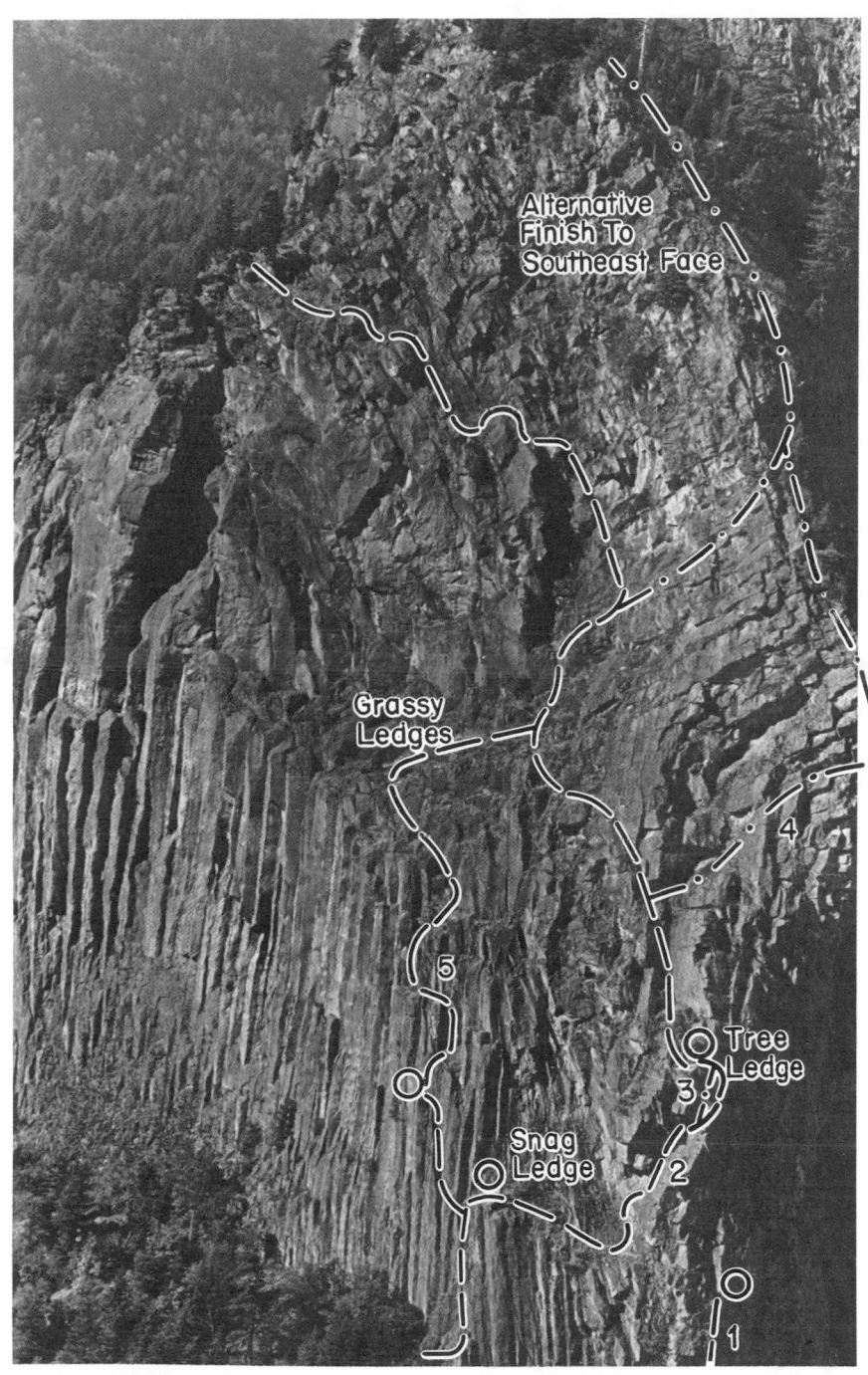

Beacon Rock from the southeast (Don Lowe photo)

face. ***Third Pitch:*** Go up past a bush in a notch, move left to the river face, mantle over a short steep wall, and you are up. Scrambling leads to the west-side trail.

5 RIGHT GULL
III, 5.10A or 5.7-AO; nuts to 2½"
There are 2 fixed pins at the start of the third pitch. Use them as your ability dictates, but leave them for the next party. ***First Pitch:*** Climb the first pitch of the Southeast Face. ***Second Pitch:*** From Snag Ledge step left and down. Climb a right-facing dihedral 80' to the top of a pinnacle. Move up to a second pinnacle on the left and belay. ***Third Pitch:*** Rappel using 2 ropes, or free or aid a short section to a ledge. Gain another ledge 25' above via 1 of 2 jam cracks to the left. ***Fourth Pitch:*** Move left again and climb another jam crack to a ledge. Step right and climb a right-facing dihedral to Grassy Ledges.

6 WRONG GULL
II, 5.10C; nuts to 2"
After stemming the lower dihedral, climb the left side of the Left Gull pinnacle to the rappel point where Right and Left Gull meet.

7 SEAGULL
II, 5.10D; nuts to 1½"
Protect high on Wrong Gull to cover the first moves of the second pitch.

8 LEFT GULL
III, 5.10A or 5.8-A0; nuts to 2½"
First Pitch: Climb a shallow dihedral immediately to the right of a tunnel. After gaining a ledge, move up and right over a short pinnacle and belay. ***Second Pitch:*** Climb a jam crack on the right 40' to a small belay ledge. ***Third Pitch:*** Move right and down a bit into a chimney using a hidden bucket. Squeeze up the chimney 50' to where it joins the Right Gull. ***Fourth and Fifth Pitches:*** Climb the last 2 pitches of Right Gull or rappel off.

9 BLUEBIRD
II, 5.10A or B; nuts to 4"
The crux is a thin finger crack and stemming problem with good protection.

10 *Variation I:* BLUEBIRD DIRECT
5.10C; nuts to 2½"
Good stemming but poorly protected.

11 *Variation II:* SUFFICIENTLY BREATHLESS
5.9; pins and nuts to ¾"
Stemming with poor protection.

12 *Variation III*
5.9; nuts to 2½"
A hand/fist crack with good protection.

13 BLOWNOUT
II, 5.10A; nuts to 2½", triples in 1¾"
Excellent protection with every type of jamming imaginable.

14 *Variation:* SECOND WIND
5.11D; nuts to 2"
Twenty feet up the second pitch of Blownout, traverse right to the next dihedral. Climb to the top.

15 THE GRUNGE BOOK
III, 5.6-A2

16 WILD TURKEYS
III, 5.6-A3; nuts and pins to 1½"

17 SMOOTH DANCER
III, 5.9-A2; nuts and pins to 1½"
The last 2 pitches have excellent free climbing.

18 DIRTY DOUBLE OVERHANG
III, 5.7-A3; nuts and pins to 2"
Most of the climb can be done with nuts.

19 TAKE FIST
III, 5.10D; nuts to 2"
The bottom pitch is dirty. The top 2 pitches are beautiful with overwhelming exposure. Rappel from the top of the third pitch with 2 ropes.

20 DIAGONAL DESPERATION
I, 5.10D-A0; nuts and pins to 2"
This climb starts on a higher tier of cliffs left of Grassy Ledges. It has not yet gone free.

Left half of South Face

21 RIVERSIDE

I, 5.10A or B; nuts to 2½″

An excellent climb which starts on a higher tier of cliffs left of Grassy Ledges.

22 FLYING SWALLOW

III, 5.10D; double set of nuts ⅛″ to 2½″

Start next to the third 2′-high tunnel. *First Pitch:* Face climb up and left past a dead snag to a crack system; follow it up and left 30′. Step right and diagonal up and right over several columns until a small ledge system leads to a semi-hanging stance off 2 bolts and a fixed pin. *Second Pitch:* Move up 5′, then continue right 15′ around a buttress.

Right half of South Face (Shari Nelson photos)

Stem the dihedral above to a sloping belay stance. **Third Pitch:** Climb an overhanging thin crack 60′ to an excellent belay. **Fourth Pitch:** Follow a hand crack to good ledges. Walk off right to Grassy Ledges or continue up a short off width to a good belay stance. **Fifth Pitch:** Rappel the route or step left and follow Dod's Jam to the west-side trail. The second pitch is difficult to protect but is worth doing if you are feeling good.

23 Variation

5.10B; duplicate set of nuts 1″ to 2½″

Climb the right-hand crack to the excellent belay on the third pitch. Protect the first series of moves by a nut placed high in the left-hand crack.

Climb the first pitch of Flying Swallow to gain access to the following 4 climbs.

24 FLIGHT TIME
II, 5.11C; nuts to 1½"

Good protection but physically difficult to place.

25 FLYING CIRCUS
III, 5.10C; duplicate set of nuts ⅛" to ¾", one each to 4"

Thirty foot run-out at the bottom of the second pitch; 165' rope required.

26 BLOOD, SWEAT, AND SMEARS
II, 5.10C; duplicate set of nuts ⅛" to ¾", one each to 2"

Good protection but a 165' rope is required. This route ends at Big Ledge. Rappel Dod's Jam.

27 TRUE GRUNT
II, 5.11A; 3 to 4 smaller pins, nuts to 1¾"

A 165' rope is required.

28 STEPPENWOLF
IV, 5.11-A0; duplicate set of nuts ⅛" to 1", one each to 2"

The first 2 pitches to Big Ledge (5.10C) have become very popular. The upper pitches above Big Ledge (5.11-A0) have yet to go free.

29 DOD'S JAM
III, 5.10B; nuts to 2½"

THE classic climb on Beacon Rock. Start next to the third 2'-high tunnel. *First Pitch:* Face climb up and left past a dead snag to a crack system; follow it up and left 120' to a tiny belay stance. *Second Pitch:* Jam, stem, or layback the overhanging off width to the top of a pillar. Follow the crack above to Big Ledge. *Third Pitch:* Walk right around the prominent buttress above Big Ledge. Climb a hand/fist crack to an alcove. Continue over an overhang and face climb up and right to a belay stance. *Fourth Pitch:* Rappel to easy ledges which lead to Grassy Ledges or climb either of 2 overhangs on the right and left sides of the amphitheater above. Belay below a thin crack higher up. *Fifth Pitch:* Climb either the thin crack directly above the belay or the off width on the left. Descend the west-side trail.

30 *Variation I:* DOD'S DEVIATION
5.9; nuts to 3″
An off width to the right of the second pitch.

31 *Variation II:* DASTARDLY CRACK
5.9; nuts to 2″
A quick and entertaining way to get off Big Ledge without rappelling.

32 *Variation III:* SQUEEZE BOX
5.10B; nuts to 2″
A popular climb, and justifiably so. The crux is a fist crack through a roof.

33 FREE FOR ALL
I, 5.8; nuts to 1¾″
Excellent protection and climb.

34 FREE FOR SOME
I, 5.11A; nuts to 1¾″
Excellent protection and climb, if you like painful, thin cracks.

35 PIPELINE
I, 5.11B; nuts to 1½″
A very difficult thin finger crack.

36 UPDRAFT TO HEAVEN
III, 5.10D-A1; nuts to 6″ and 6 to 7 knifeblades
A 15′ section of this climb has yet to be led free. The first pitch follows a slab 20′ to the right of the ridge which leads up to Jensen's.

37 JENSEN'S RIDGE
III, 5.10C; nuts to 4″, duplicate set from 1¾″up
The finger crack is the technical crux, but some find the off width above to be the psychological crux.

38 *Variation:* MOSTLY AIR
5.10B; nuts to 2½″
Poorly protected.

39 LAY LADY LAY
III, 5.10B; nuts to 2½″

Excellent protection and climb. Unfortunately, poison oak grows up the bottom of the climb every year.

40 RIP CITY
II, 5.10A or B; nuts to 1¾″

Great climb except it has the same problem as Lay Lady Lay.

41 HARD TIMES
II, 5.10B; nuts to 2½″

Pure stemming and good protection.

42 RAGTIME
II, 5.10C; nuts to 2½″

Excellent protection and climb.

43 BOULDER PROBLEM IN THE SKY
II, 5.10D; nuts to 2½″

Some think the stemming at the start of the crux pitch is more difficult than the roof, yet everyone falls off at the roof.

44 *Variation*
5.9; nuts to 2½″

From the top of the crux pitch, follow grungy slabs straight up rather than a double hand crack up the side of the left buttress.

45 ON THE MOVE
II, 5.10D-A0; nuts to 4″ and 3 knifeblades

Has yet to go free.

Opposite, West Face (Shari Nelson photo)

4 SMITH ROCK

A variety of climbs, better than average weather, and accessibility make Smith Rock the best rock climbing area in Oregon. But Smith Rock is more than a rock gymnasium. The surrounding environment of castellated spires, winding river, and distant Cascade peaks are an integral part of the climbing experience. You do not have to be a climber to appreciate Smith Rock, but being a climber makes it a very special place.

Smith Rock is located 6 miles north of Redmond and 3 miles east of U.S. 97 in Central Oregon. From Terrebonne on U.S. 97, follow state park signs to a day-use area overlooking the Crooked River Gorge. A trail then leads down into the gorge, where a footbridge provides access to the opposite shore.

The greater part of Smith Rock is owned by the Oregon State Parks and Recreation Branch of the Department of Transportation. The branch currently maintains an "overnight bivouac" area for park users. The bivouac area is located on a bench west of the day-use area. It is reached by following a footpath which leads from the southern end of the parking area. Two portable toilets have been set up next to the bivouac area. Other facilities can be found at the day-use area. A fee of $1 is charged per person per night. Open fires are not recommended. Further questions about park facilities should be directed to the full-time ranger who lives in a trailer between Juniper Junction and the main parking area.

The rock at Smith Rock is welded tuff which consolidated from molten ash 30 million years ago. Welded tuff is extremely soft and often rotten. A stiff wind has been known to blow away handholds. This can be unnerving for the uninitiated, but is certainly no worse than climbing in other soft-rock climbing areas. Most of the cracks have been cleaned out, and once you gain confidence climbing in the nubbins that abound, you can do some fascinating climbing.

Legend has it that it never rains at Smith Rock. The fact is that the surrounding area averages 10" of rain a year. Since the majority falls in December and January, climbing season is usually February through November.

Climbers have clearly had a detrimental impact on Smith Rock in the past. The following guidelines are helpful:

1. Stay on established trails. Pictures taken before 1973 show very little hillside erosion. The more popular areas now exhibit glaring scars, all of it created by indiscriminate hiking. Efforts are being made to restore vegetation and construct a formal trail system. Please respect these efforts and stay on trails.
2. If you suspect or know a bird of prey is nesting on a route, refrain from climbing there.

3. Do not camp in the Crooked River Canyon.
4. Respect the privacy of those who live in the area, and never cross their property without permission.
5. Large groups such as climbing classes should minimize their impact on the terrain by using the basalt rims above the Crooked River for instruction.

Basalt Rim or Beginners' Areas

Lining the Crooked River are basalt cliffs ranging in height from 2' to 200'. The largest cliffs are on private land and climbing should not be attempted there. However, excellent smaller cliffs offer convenient leading or top-rope problems. The best area lies on the point of land across the Crooked River from the Monument. Another fine cliff exists just south of the old climbers' camp on the east side of the river. Both areas provide an ideal place to bring large groups to keep their impact on the park and other people at a minimum. There are no formal names or grades; just pick a crack and try it. Nuts will suffice for most climbs.

Picnic Lunch Wall

The large wall directly above the Crooked River footbridge is called Picnic Lunch Wall.

1 SCORPIO

II, 5.8; nuts to 2½"

Hike up to the far right side of Picnic Lunch Wall. Rope up on a large boulder underneath a right-facing crack. *First Pitch:* Climb the crack to a belay ledge. *Second Pitch:* Gain a crack system above, either by face climbing straight up from the belay, or face climbing to the right and then back left to the crack. (Neither alternative can be protected, but the right side is relatively simple.) Continue up cracks to an alcove. *Third Pitch:* Climb over a chockstone, being careful not to dump it into your praying belayer. Continue to the top. Descend Misery Ridge.

2 *Variation:* I LOST MY LUNCH

5.9

Instead of traversing back to the left on the second pitch, face climb right 10', then follow loose blocks straight up to a left-facing corner. After belaying, continue to the top. This variation is 180' long, extremely dangerous, and unprotected.

3 FOOL'S OVERTURE

II, 5.9; nuts to 1½"

Start just to the left of Scorpio in a rotten open book. *First Pitch:* Climb

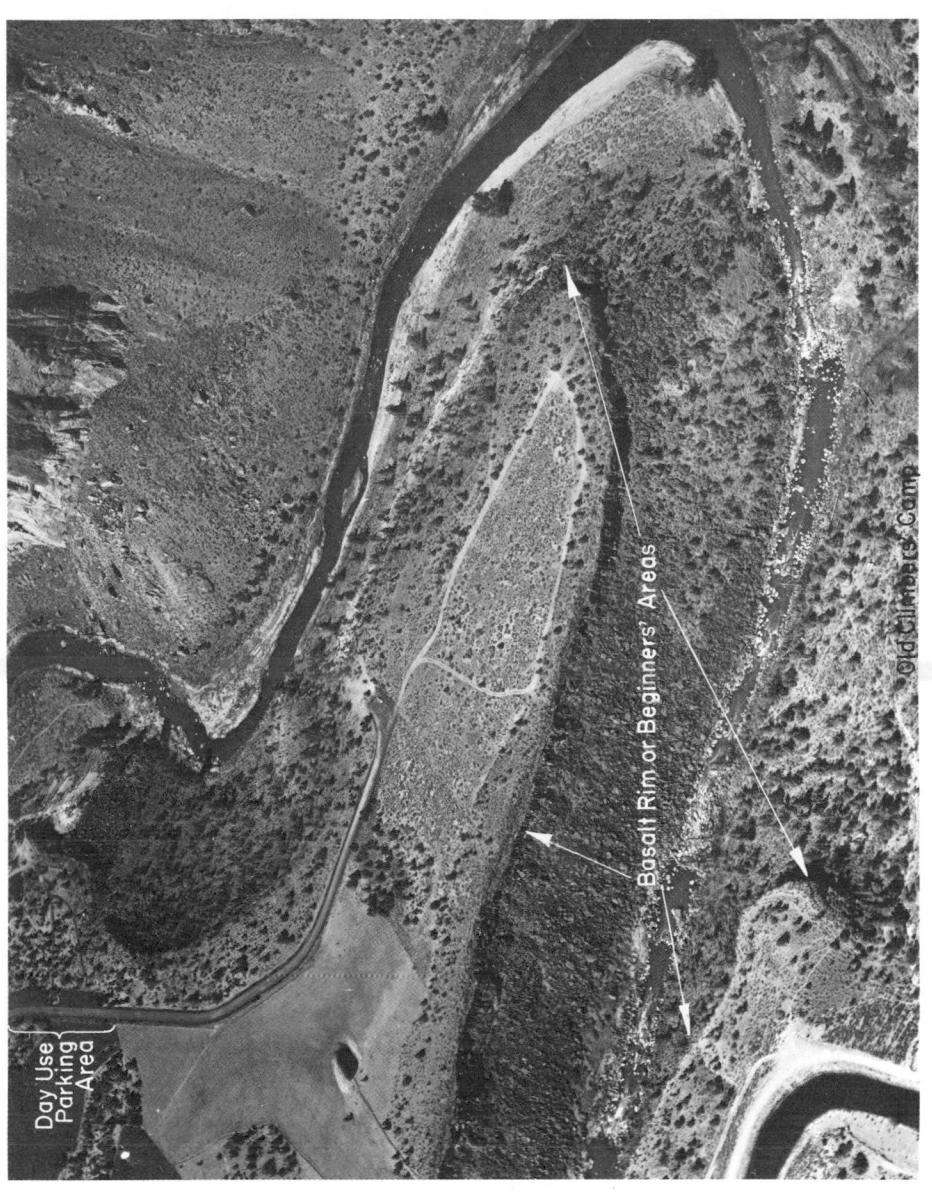

Basalt Rim along the Crooked River (Oregon Department of Transportation photo)

the rotten open book, and from the top, traverse left. Climb straight up 60' of unprotected (but easy) face climbing to a ledge. Climb past 2 bolts to the top of a ramp. Follow an indistinct crack up and right to a belay ledge. A 165' rope is required. *Second Pitch:* Step right and face climb straight up to a right-facing open book. Follow the open book to a belay on a sloping ledge. *Third Pitch:* Drop down and face climb left to a gully system leading to the top. Descend Misery Ridge.

4 NO PICNIC

II, 5.10D; nuts to 3"

First Pitch: Climb the obvious alcove between Free Lunch and Fool's Overture to a short dihedral (crux). When the dihedral ends, climb left and up across a knobby face (bolt protection) to the first belay ledge. *Second Pitch:* A few loose face moves straight up lead to a crack that is followed 30' to a small roof. Climb right onto a red face to avoid bad rock. Climb up 15', then left to a belay below an ominous chimney. *Third Pitch:* The surprisingly easy and well-protected chimney is climbed until it is possible to exit right onto a large ledge. A short headwall is climbed to a larger belay ledge. *Fourth Pitch:* Wander off right to the top.

5 *Variation:* FARMERS' VARIATION

5.10A

Rather than exiting right on the third pitch, plow directly up miserable rock to the top of the chimney. Generally done only by those unfortunate enough to get off the route.

6 FREE LUNCH

III, 5.10A; nuts to 2"

Free Lunch defies the Fourth Law of Ecology, which states: "There is no such thing as a free lunch." Begin about 100' right of twin arches at the base of some large potholes. *First Pitch:* Climb to the top of the potholes. Face climb up and left around a right-facing corner (crux). Continue up and left to the top of a pinnacle. *Second Pitch:* Traverse left, climb up and down another pinnacle, and continue face climbing left to a large ledge. *Third, Fourth and Fifth Pitches:* Climb the crack system above to the top.

7 *Variation:* UNFINISHED SYMPHONY

IV, 5.9-A3 or 5.12B-A3

The original line of ascent, which gains the upper 3 pitches via 2 pitches up the twin arches. The first pitch has been done free.

Opposite, Picnic Lunch Wall (Don Lowe photo)

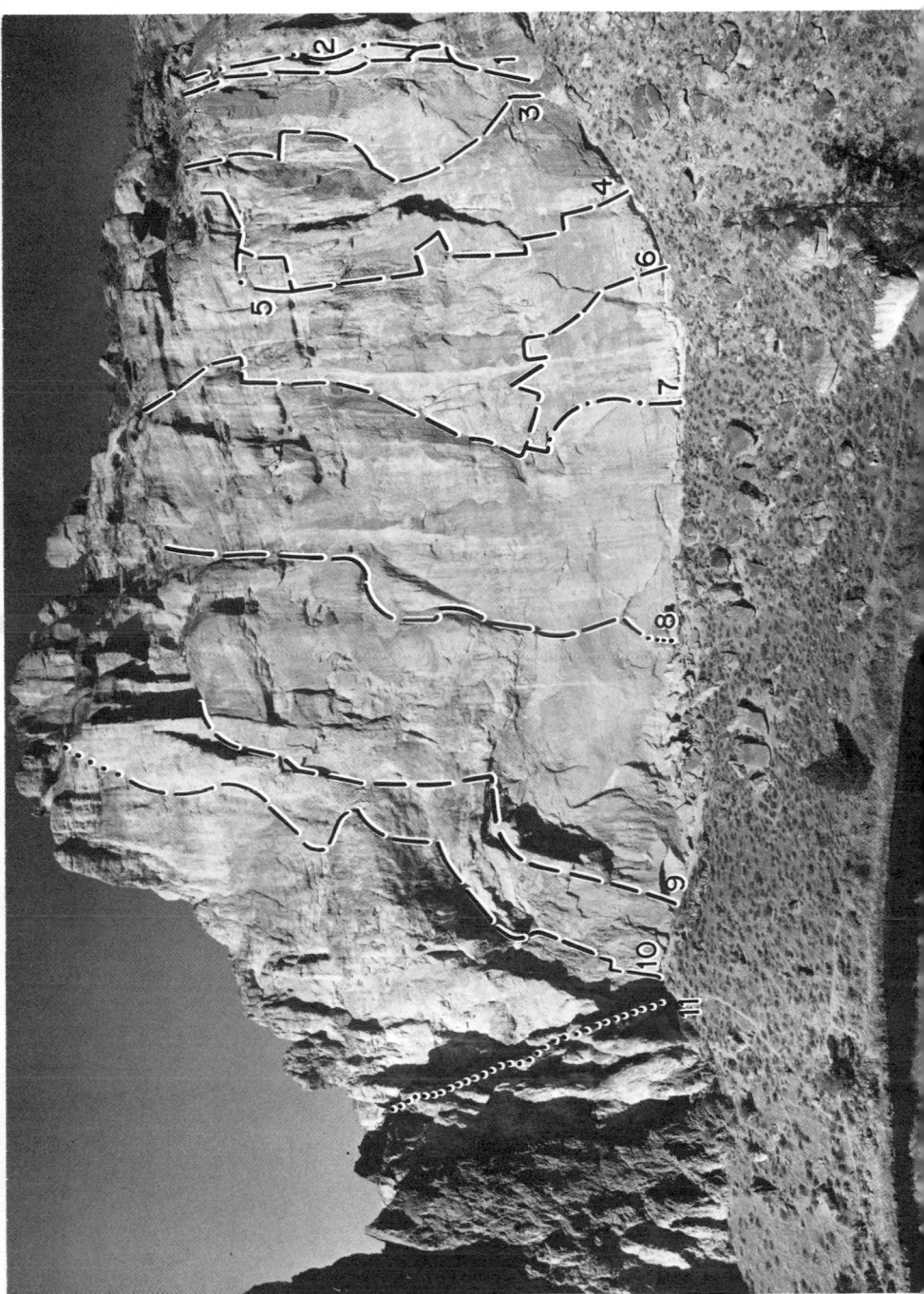

8 SOFT SHOE BALLET
V, 5.10A-A5; protection unknown

A difficult and dangerous aid climb with definite groundfall probability on the first pitch. See the photograph of Picnic Lunch Wall for the line of ascent.

9 PICNIC LUNCH WALL
V, 5.6-A4; protection unknown

During the early seventies, Picnic Lunch Wall was a very difficult and dangerous climb. It is much easier and safer today due to the addition of numerous bolts. See the photograph of Picnic Lunch Wall for the line of ascent.

10 JOURNEY TO IXTLAN
V, 5.10A-A4; hooks to #4 Friends

See the photograph of Picnic Lunch Wall for the line of ascent.

Ship Rock

A large spire adjoining the left side of Picnic Lunch Wall. The rock is probably the worst at Smith Rock. Ship Rock was originally called the Red Fin.

11 EAST CHIMNEY
II, 5.6

Not recommended for the casual 5.6 climber. The climb starts below the col between Picnic Lunch Wall and Ship Rock in a large chimney. Follow the chimney to its end at the col. Rappel down West Gully to descend.

12 WEST GULLY
II, 5.6; nuts to 1″

A climber selecting this rotten route would do well to wear a suit of armor as well as a hard hat. Climb to the notch between Picnic Lunch Wall and Ship Rock using a gully on the west side. Follow the north ridge of the Red Fin to the top, keeping to the right (west) side of the ridge. Rappel the route to descend.

Table Scraps Wall

From the Crooked River footbridge, follow the main trail along the Crooked River as it curves west around Ship Rock. After passing Ship

Rock, hike up a steep hillside to an indistinct lump known as Table Scraps Wall.

13 CITY DUMP
II, 5.7; nuts to 2½ "

First Pitch: On the right side of the cliff, climb cracks to a ledge at the base of a slab. *Second Pitch:* Follow a crack up the slab to the spot where the slab lies back. *Third Pitch:* Continue up easy slabs to the base of a crack which leads to the top of the cliff. Descend a gully on the left.

14 VANISHING UNCERTAINTY
I, 5.9; nuts to 1½ "

Climb an obvious face crack in the middle of Table Scraps Wall to low-angle slabs. Descend a gully on the left.

15 WASTE LAND
I, 5.8; nuts to 4"

Waste Land follows a right-facing corner on the far left side of Table Scraps Wall. Descend a gully on the left.

Wooden Ships

The 2 large rock formations close to the trail after Ship Rock are called Wooden Ships.

16 SHIPWRECK
II, 5.9; nuts to 2½ "

This climb has nothing to offer but lousy rock and a constant rain of debris from above. *First Pitch:* Climb 20' up a right-facing dihedral with excellent orange rock. Traverse left and down into a groove. Climb the groove and loose boulder piles above to Avalanche Ledge. *Second Pitch:* Climb a squeeze chimney to the top. Descend off the left side of the formation using a chimney.

17 SOLAR
II, 5.9; nuts to 2½ "

Start in the gully on the east side of the second buttress. *First Pitch:* Traverse horizontally onto the south face of the buttress until you reach a left-facing dihedral. Follow it to an idyllic belay ledge. *Second Pitch:* Follow a left-facing overhanging dihedral to the top. *Third Pitch:* Scramble along the top and left side of the buttress to descend.

18 *Variation:* NO-DOZ

II, A4

Start at the very bottom of the buttress and aid up a decomposed crack to the spot where it joins Solar.

19 COCAINE CRACK

I, 5.11B; nuts to 2½″ (not shown)

An arching discontinuous crack system splits the steep western face of the Solar buttress. Scramble up an easy chimney to the base of the crack. A strenuous pitch, which combines hard crack and face climbing with what one climber called "wild Kung Fu stemming," leads to a ledge. Rappel.

Morning Glory Wall

Morning Glory Wall is just to the left of Wooden Ships, and is distinguished by 2 huge dihedrals.

20 LION'S CHAIR

III, 5.11A; nuts to 2½″, mostly small wires

Start in a 170′ left-facing dihedral which ends at a roof. A juniper grows immediately to the right of the dihedral. ***First and Second Pitches:*** Climb the dihedral to the roof. Skirt warily to the right around a loose block, and face climb up and left to bolts. ***Third Pitch:*** Face climbing up and left leads to a sloping corner. Follow the corner to a bolt belay. ***Fourth Pitch:*** Move up a spectacular flake crack to a large ledge. ***Fifth Pitch:*** A short pitch leads to the top. A very good climb which protects much more easily with the newer nuts.

21 *Variation*

5.7

After clearing the roof on the second pitch, make your escape horizontally to the right, to ledges and an easy descent.

22 ZEBRA

II, 5.10A or 5.9; nuts to 2½″

Begin in colossal potholes at the base of a huge right-facing book. ***First Pitch:*** Follow potholes up and right to a bolt belay. ***Second Pitch:*** Storm roof above. The difficulty depends on how it is stormed. Follow a crack for 60′ to a belay ledge. ***Third Pitch:*** Continue to follow the crack until it ends on a pedestal. ***Fourth Pitch:*** Move left and follow chimneys and gullies to the top.

Opposite, Table Scraps Wall to Cinnamon Slab from the south (Don Lowe photo)

23 *Variation I:* ORIGINAL START
5.12

Climb a left-arching seam to the right of the potholes. A top-rope problem which has never been led.

24 *Variation II:* ZEBRA DIRECT
5.10D

Start directly below the first belay and face climb straight up past 2 bolts to join the first pitch.

25 *Variation III:* ZION
5.9

From the end of the second pitch, follow the crack until it looks possible to face climb right. Traverse horizontally right to a shallow crack. Climb the crack to the spot where it joins Lion's Chair.

26 LION'S JAW
I, 5.8; nuts to 1½″

Locate a right-facing dihedral on the left side of Morning Glory Wall. *First Pitch:* Climb the dihedral to a ledge. *Second and Third Pitches:* Climb a miserable rotten chimney to the top.

27 *Variation*
5.7

A squeeze chimney on the left can also be used to gain the first belay. The chimney on the last 2 pitches is an evil affair where the leader might exchange a wide variety of loose rock for curses from below. Better to avoid such an exchange and rappel off.

The Peanut

Between the Fourth Horseman and Morning Glory Wall is a large boulder. There are 2 routes on this boulder, **28 POP GOES THE NUBBIN** (I, 5.9) and **29 PEANUT BRITTLE** (I, 5.8). Bolts are in place on both routes and are the only protection required.

Rope-de-Dope Rock (not shown)

A large squat boulder of welded tuff sits across the river from Morning Glory Wall. Several short but excellent top-rope or lead problems can be found, making it an ideal place for classes and mountain rescue groups.

The Fourth Horseman

To the left of Morning Glory Wall is a large face with several cracks. The face culminates in a spire called the Fourth Horseman. The remaining 3 horsemen are smaller spires on the ridge above the Fourth Horseman. Descent for all the climbs on this formation is usually down the Cinnamon Slab rappel. (See route 39.)

30 FRIDAY'S JINX

I, 5.7; nuts to 1½"

Friday's Jinx follows a left-facing dihedral on the right side of the Fourth Horseman. *First Pitch:* Traverse right from a high point at the base of the cliff. Climb delicately over an overhang and up a crack to a large block. Belay bolts are in place, but nuts would be nice as a backup. *Second Pitch:* Follow the left-facing dihedral to the top.

31 *Variation I*

5.10A

Instead of traversing right on the first pitch, climb a right-facing dihedral to the first belay.

32 *Variation II*

5.7

From the first belay, traverse right and down, then follow a right-facing corner to the top.

33 CRACK OF INFINITY

I, 5.10A; nuts to 2"

First Pitch: Follow a thin crack which starts below the roof on Calamity Jam and diagonals up and right to the Friday's Jinx belay. *Second Pitch:* Jam an exposed face crack to the left of the Friday's Jinx dihedral. Belay below an overhanging crack. *Third Pitch:* Climb the overhanging crack to the top.

34 CALAMITY JAM

I, 5.10C; nuts to 1½"

Climb a long thin crack which splits the river face. The crack is perfectly straight except for an arching overhang at the bottom. An excellent climb.

The Fourth Horseman (Shari Nelson photo)

35 PACK ANIMAL

I, 5.8; nuts to 2″

The obvious right-facing dihedral on the left side of the Fourth Horseman is split in two. The regular route avoids trouble by face climbing to the upper dihedral from the left. After belay bolts, climb the remaining dihedral to the top.

36 *Variation*

5.10B

Confront trouble by climbing the bottom dihedral.

Cinnamon Slab Area

To the left of the Fourth Horseman is a low-angle slab with **37** and **38 UNNAMED CLIMBS.** The difficulty of both climbs is about 5.4. Descend via the Cinnamon Slab rappel.

The Dihedrals

The Dihedrals has also been called the Bookends. Both names aptly fit the sharply defined outside corners and dihedrals that make up the geometric beauty of this section of cliff.

39 CINNAMON SLAB

I, 5.6; nuts to 3″

A fixed rappel for the Dihedrals area is located at the top of Cinnamon Slab. Start at the base of a narrow ramp which slants up and right. *First Pitch:* Climb up ramp 60′ to a large, accommodating ledge. *Second Pitch:* Clear a small bulge just above the ledge and follow a crack to the top.

40 *Variation:* CINNAMON TOAST

5.7 (not shown)

After clearing the bulge at the start of the second pitch, step left and climb a steep face to the top.

41 KARATE CRACK TO THE PEAPOD

I, 5.10A; nuts to 3″ (not shown)

This is a Smith Rock classic. A hand crack immediately left of Cinnamon Slab which intersects a peapod-shaped chimney via a horizontal crack. *First Pitch:* Jam crack and hand traverse into the Peapod. *Second Pitch:* Chimney up the Peapod and exit right to the Cinnamon Slab belay.

42 TATOR TOTS
I, 5.10A; bolt protection

Begin downhill from Karate Crack on the right side of the buttress separating Cinnamon Slab from Upper Ceiling. *First Pitch:* Climb up and left to a small alcove on the river face of the buttress. Follow the line of least resistance over a bulge and halfway up the buttress to a bolt belay. Except for the crux, the first pitch is poorly protected. *Second Pitch:* Climb past bolts to the top.

43 *Variation I:* KAROT TOTS
5.11C

Climb Karate Crack to within 6' of the hand traverse. Face climb up and left following an incipient crack to the first belay on Tator Tots. A superb route which was originally done on aid and called Euclid's Column.

44 *Variation II*
5.11 to 5.12

Rather than beginning the first pitch on the right side of the buttress, start at the bottom. Boulder over a large overhang to reach the first bolt. The difficulty varies with the route chosen to clear the overhang.

45 UPPER CEILING
I, 5.7; nuts to 3″

Start below a large recessed chimney capped by an overhang. Follow the chimney to a good belay under the overhang. Some climbers will be small enough to squeeze through. If not, going around the outside of the roof is not as bad as it looks.

46 *Variation*
5.7 (not shown)

About 30' up the chimney, switch to a crack on the right face and climb it until it rejoins the regular route.

47 SUNSHINE DIHEDRAL
I, 5.12A; triple set of nuts ¼″ to ¾″

The first of 2 large right-facing dihedrals. A beautiful route with good protection.

48 MOONSHINE DIHEDRAL
I, 5.9; nuts to 1¼″

The second of 2 large right-facing dihedrals. There are 2 pitches, but most climbers avoid rotten rock on the second pitch by rappelling from bolts 70' up.

Opposite, the Dihedrals (Shari Nelson photo)

49 RATTLESNAKE CHIMNEY

I, 5.6; nuts to 3"

A deep chimney with a large chockstone, around the corner from Moonshine Dihedral. Stem up the chimney past the chockstone to a wide belay ledge. Continue up easy ground to the top. The climb was named for an unexpected encounter on the second ascent.

50 BOOKWORM

I, 5.7; nuts to 3½"

A 2" to 4" crack left of Rattlesnake Chimney, ending 40' up on a pedestal. More people have fallen out of the first moves than have not. If you manage those, you've got it made—at least until the second pitch. *First Pitch:* Follow the crack to the top of the pedestal. *Second Pitch:* Face climb (poor protection) up and left into a dihedral. Follow the dihedral past a bolt to the top.

51 METHUSELAH'S COLUMN

I, 5.9; nuts to 2", bolt protection

A buttress immediately left of Bookworm that is filled with fascinating Smith Rock nubbins. *First Pitch:* Gain a belay ledge halfway up the buttress by climbing the initial half of Bookworm or Lycopodophyta, or face climb directly up the buttress. Protection is difficult to find if you choose the buttress. *Second Pitch:* Attack the last half of the buttress using ¼" bolt protection. Watch out for portable handholds.

52 LYCOPODOPHYTA

I, 5.8; nuts to 2"

Lycopodophyta is a small dihedral which leads up to a chimney near the top of the cliff. The climb can be done in one lead but is best when broken into 2 pitches.

53 DETERIORATA

I, 5.8; nuts to 1½"

Deteriorata is a single-pitch climb which follows the last dihedral on the left side of the Dihedrals area.

The Christian Brothers—East Side

The Christian Brothers is a narrow group of pinnacles separating the Dihedrals area from the Smith Summit group. From north to south, the summits include the teetering Abbot, the Friar, the Pope, the twin spires of the Monk, and the Priest.

54 AIR TO SPARE

II, 5.10A-A5

Begin at the base of an overhanging wall to the right of Shoes of the Fisherman. *First Pitch:* Follow discontinuous seams and bolts 60' to 2 bolts. Continue up a knifeblade crack to a belay "hole." *Second Pitch:* Free left, then aid another knifeblade crack which leads to the top.

55 SHOES OF THE FISHERMAN

II, 5.11B; nuts to 2¾", include three 1¾"

Two parallel overhanging cracks slice the east face of the Friar. The right crack is Shoes of the Fisherman. *First Pitch:* Climb to the base of a large overhang. Work out and move up into a beautiful hand crack. Follow the crack 70' to a bolt belay. *Second Pitch:* The second pitch is a pile of rubble. It is well worth rappelling rather than climbing up.

56 WARTLEY'S REVENGE

II, 5.11B; nuts to 1½"

Two parallel overhanging cracks slice the east face of the Friar. The left crack is Wartley's Revenge. *First Pitch:* Climb 70' to a small ledge (crux). *Second Pitch:* Continue up the crack to a semi-hanging bolt belay. *Third Pitch:* Layback up to a large ledge. Climb into a gully (the Hobbit Hole) between the Friar and the Abbot. *Fourth Pitch:* Climb out of the gully on the north side and contour around the east side of the Abbot. Walk to the Cinnamon Slab rappel.

57 THE BEARD

I, 5.6 or 5.7; nuts to 1¾"

A small flake at the bottom of the Friar, which can be climbed on the right side (5.7) or left side (5.6).

The following 4 climbs reach the top of an indistinct pinnacle on the flank of the Friar. Descend off a bolt rappel at the top.

58 GOLGOTHA

I, 5.11A or 5.11C; nuts to ¾"

Climb 15' up the left side of the Beard, then follow a thin left-leaning crack in a shallow corner past several bolts. Belay atop New Testament. The crux of this challenging line involves a long reach. The shorter your reach, the harder the climb.

59 *Variation:* TEMPTATION
5.10A

Midway up Golgotha, it is possible to traverse left on face holds past a bolt to New Testament.

60 NEW TESTAMENT
I, 5.9 or 5.10A; nuts to 2"

A good climb which follows a prominent face crack on the right side of the pinnacle. Religious use of face holds will overcome a vanishing crack near the top.

61 REVELATIONS
I, 5.9; bolt protection

Follow face holds on the edge of the Old Testament face, past several bolts. Belay atop New Testament.

62 OLD TESTAMENT
I, 5.7; nuts to 2"

Climb a crack on the left side of the pinnacle. Traverse right and follow a second crack to the top. Loose in some spots, but not dangerously so.

63 HEATHENS' HIGHWAY
II, 5.10A; nuts to 3", bolt protection

First Pitch: Climb Golgotha, New Testament, Revelations, or Old Testament. *Second Pitch:* Climb a rotten pedestal on the left, strike up and right, then back left on the wall above (crux). *Third Pitch:* Move right 10', then climb the crack above to a belay in a chimney between the Pope and the Friar. *Fourth Pitch:* Grunge up the rotten flank of the Friar to the top. *Fifth Pitch:* Rappel the northeast face of the Friar and boulder around the east side of the Abbot.

64 GOTHIC CATHEDRAL
II, 5.8; nuts to 3"

The name is beautiful; the climb is rotten and ugly. Start on the east side of the Christian Brothers in a large chimney separating the Monk and the Friar. *First Pitch:* Chimney about 100' through an overhang to a large loose block. *Second Pitch:* Gain the top of the Pope by climbing the right-hand crack of 2 parallel cracks. *Third Pitch:* Rappel or climb over the Friar and around the Abbot. (See Christian Brothers Traverse.)

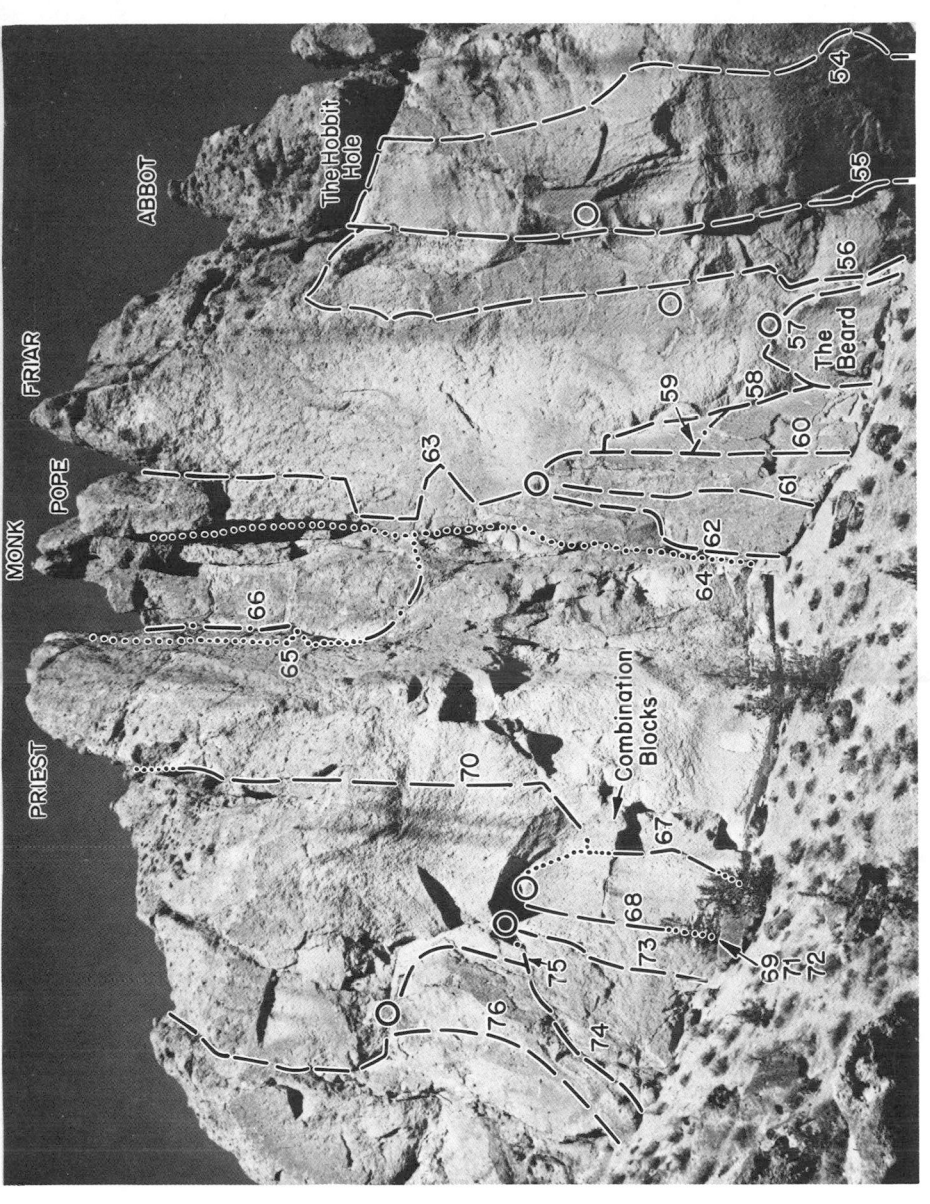

The Christian Brothers—East Side (Shari Nelson photo)

65 *Variation I:* LAST GASP

5.9

From the first belay, traverse left on rotten rock to the base of a large crack splitting the Priest. Gasp up the crack to the summit shoulder of the Priest (poor protection). If you are still interested in climbing rotten rock, go to the summit of the Priest; otherwise, rappel down the west side of the Priest.

66 *Variation II:* SAFETY VALVE

5.7

About 30' up the crack on Last Gasp, escape to the right up a sloping dihedral. Climb over the Friar and around the Abbot. (See Christian Brothers Traverse.)

Combination Blocks

Below the Priest, on the east side of the Christian Brothers, are 2 large blocks. When seen from below, the top block lies sideways on the bottom block. Only one rope is needed to rappel from the top.

67 CHARLIE'S CHIMNEY

I, 5.6; nuts to 3″

Follow the right side of the bottom block and tunnel under the top block.

68 TINKER TOY

I, 5.8; nuts to 3″

Climb the left outside edge of the blocks. Poor protection.

69 THE BOWLING ALLEY

I, 5.4; nuts to 3″ (not shown)

Climb a crack/chimney system formed by the main wall and inside left edge of the blocks.

70 DOUBLE STAIN

II, A2

From the right side of the top of Combination Blocks, follow bolts leading right to a crack. Follow the crack to the top. Rappel down the west side of the Priest.

71 TOYS IN THE ATTIC
I, 5.9; nuts to 3½" (not shown)

Begin 6' to the left of Combination Blocks. Climb a hand/fist crack to the base of a large roof. Traverse left to a bolt belay. Rappel.

72 *Variation:* CHILD'S PLAY
5.10C (not shown)

Two-thirds of the way up Toys in the Attic, follow a thin crack up and left to the belay bolts.

73 HESITATION BLUES
I, 5.10B; nuts to 2", fixed pins

This is a fun route. Begin below a thin face crack about 10' to the left of Toys in the Attic. Climb the thin crack to belay bolts. Rappel.

74 TOY BLOCKS
I, 5.10A; nuts to 2½"

The blocks seem loose and probably are, but they have resisted several attempts to pull them off. Between Dancer and Combination Blocks is a hand crack which traverses from left to right. Climb the crack to the base of some large blocks. Climb over the blocks and up to the Dancer belay. Rappel.

75 *Variation:* SELF-PRESERVATION VARIATION
5.10A

Instead of climbing the blocks, continue to traverse right as far as the rappel bolts for Toys in the Attic.

76 DANCER
I, 5.8; bolt protection, nuts to 3" for the second pitch

Forty feet to the left of Combination Blocks is a knobby face. Dance up knobs to a ledge (5.7). Most people rappel at this point; however, it is possible to climb the left-hand crack above (5.8) to the summit shoulder of the Priest. Rappel off the west side of the Priest.

77 THE ASTERISK
I, 5.6 (not shown)

The Asterisk is a small overhanging rock immediately south of the Priest. It can be scaled on the southwest side.

Asterisk Pass

Just left of the Asterisk is a low point in the cliff where it is possible to pass from the eastern side of Smith Rock to the western side. Asterisk Pass, as it is named, is the easiest way to reach west-side climbs, including Monkey Face. The alternatives are a long but pleasant walk along the river or a short but miserable hike over Misery Ridge.

Smith Rock Group

The Smith Rock Group forms the southern end of Smith Rock State Park and is surrounded on three sides by the Crooked River. From north to south, the principal summits are Platform, Arrowpoint, and Smith Summit.

There are 2 methods of getting down from climbs in the Smith Rock Group. If you are familiar with the route and have 2 ropes, it is more convenient to use a fixed rappel down Bits and Pieces. If you are not familiar with Bits and Pieces, a long walk down the west side of the Smith Rock Group is best. To do this, hike up to the col between Platform and Arrowpoint. Contour around the west side of Arrowpoint and follow a ridge past Smith Summit. From this point, follow well-defined trails down a broad slope to a trail which returns to Asterisk Pass.

78 SKYWAYS
I, 5.10A; nuts to 6″

Large loose boulders make this a dangerous climb. Rope up at the south end of Asterisk Pass. *First Pitch:* Bulldoze up a crack on the east side of a wall, passing large loose boulders and an overhang. *Second Pitch:* Do the last pitch of Sky Ridge from a belay on the ridge.

79 SKY CHIMNEY
I, 5.7; nuts to 2½″

Rope up 100′ left of Asterisk Pass at the base of a chimney. *First Pitch:* Climb the chimney to the highest ledge on the right. *Second Pitch:* Follow a right-facing dihedral and belay in a small cubby hole under a roof. *Third Pitch:* Clear the roof and climb to the top. Be very aware of the loose rock and pea gravel at the finish, especially if there is a party below you.

80 *Variation:* BYWAYS
5.8

Start as for Skyways. Follow an upward traversing crack to the first belay of Sky Chimney.

Smith Rock Group—East Side (Shari Nelson photo)

81 WHITE SATIN
I, 5.8; nuts to 2″

First Pitch: Follow the first pitch of Sky Chimney. *Second Pitch:* Climb a crack to the left of Sky Chimney up and over a flake, then up to an alcove. *Third Pitch:* Climb up incredibly good rock, exiting either straight up or to the right.

82 BLACK VELCRO
II, 5.9; nuts to 2½″

First Pitch: Follow the first pitch of Sky Chimney. *Second Pitch:* Traverse left along scary fourth class ledges to a curving left-facing corner. *Third Pitch:* Climb the corner about 80′ to a bolt belay. *Fourth Pitch:* Continue up and right in the corner until forced to face climb right and up over a bulge. Climb a right-facing corner above to a two-bolt belay. *Fifth Pitch:* Scramble up to the top.

83 SNIBBLE TOWER
III, 5.9-C1 or III, 5.9; nuts to 2″

The beauty of the fifth pitch makes up for the squalor of the lower sections. Start at the base of a chimney on the east face of Platform. *First Pitch:* Avoid the chimney and angle left to a ledge. *Second Pitch:* Traverse back right on face holds, regain the chimney, and grunt up to some ledges. *Third Pitch:* Either free climb a rotten section from below, or use bolts arcing from right to left higher up, to gain a gully. *Fourth Pitch:* Follow the gully to a prominent ramp leading across the east face. Climb the ramp to where it ends. Belay around the corner below an overhanging corner. *Fifth Pitch:* Climb the corner to a good belay. *Sixth Pitch:* Scramble up junky rock to the top or descend south into a gully. Climb out of the gully to easy ground.

84 SMITH SUMMIT—EAST WALL AND EAST SUMMIT
III, 5.8; nuts to 2½″

The entire route is rotten, difficult to protect, and ugly. A true Oregon death tour. A difficult climb to locate using a written description. The best method is to use the photograph and a little common sense. *First Pitch:* Face climbing up and right leads to the base of a 2″ crack. *Second Pitch:* Climb the crack to a good belay. *Third Pitch:* Junk climbing leads left up a ramp 160′ to a good ledge. *Fourth Pitch:* Move right and face climb to a crack. Climb the crack and really trashy rock above to a cleft. *Fifth Pitch:* Wander over loose cow pies to the top. *Sixth Pitch:* Rappel to the amphitheater on the southeast side of Smith Summit. Scramble west up a gully to escape the amphitheater.

85 CARABID

I, 5.6; nuts to 2½"

South of Smith Summit is a large amphitheater. Scramble up into the amphitheater a short distance to gain a crack system on the left wall. The crack leads to the same rappel point as Phoenix. Use 2 ropes to descend.

86 PHOENIX

I, 5.9; nuts to 2", bolt protection

Phoenix begins just to the left of Carabid on sound red rock. Follow face holds past bolts to a ledge at the end of the good rock. Rappel using 2 ropes.

87 KUNZA KORNER

I, 5.10C; nuts to 1½" including many small wires (not shown)

Follow the river trail to the southernmost point of the Smith Rock Group. Rope up at the base of a 100' corner, and stem and face climb 80' to a rappel anchor. A beautiful climb lurking amid some of the worst rock east of the Mississippi.

88 COD ROCK—SUNSET BOULEVARD

I, 5.8; protection unknown (not shown)

An obscure formation on the west side of the Smith Rock Group, best approached via Asterisk Pass. Sunset Boulevard follows an obvious crack splitting the west face. Several other routes of about 5.6 or 5.7 difficulty have been worked out, but the rock is bad.

89 CULLS IN SPACE

I, 5.10C; nuts to 2½" (not shown)

Walk south from the west side of Asterisk Pass until the cliff base recedes from the path. A crack running from right to left in a rising traverse under an awesome roof should be apparent on the slope above. Fourth class up ledges on the right of the formation and belay immediately under the crack. Power hand jamming leads to the top.

90 ARROWPOINT

I, 3 (not shown)

A small spire just west of Smith Summit and the Platform. It is best approached by hiking up the west side of the Smith Rock Group, walking north to a level rock ridge, and following the ridge past Smith Summit. An easy scramble leads up its northwest side.

91 SHAFT
I, 5.9; nuts to 1½" (not shown)

Climb a thin crack on the north face of Arrowpoint to easier climbing and the summit. A very short but okay climb.

92 PLATFORM—SOUTH ARETE
I, 4 (not shown)

Approach as for Arrowpoint, but continue around the west side of Arrowpoint and down the slope. Climb the south ridge of the Platform to the summit.

93 SMITH SUMMIT—WEST SUMMIT
I, A1; bow and arrow, ropes of various sizes (not shown)

Smith Summit is a misnomer. There are in fact 2 summits, and it is not possible (at least so far) to climb from one to the other. East Wall reaches the top of the eastern summit. The western summit was ascended by shooting an arrow with a thin line over the top, dragging a thicker rope over and prusiking.

94 NO BRAIN, NO PAIN
II, 5.10D; nuts to 2" (not shown)

A beautiful single-pitch climb; unfortunately, there are 3 pitches. Walk 150' right on the west side of Asterisk Pass to the base of a huge 40' boulder resting against the wall. *First Pitch:* Climb the easy chimney behind the boulder to a large ledge. Walk up a ramp to the right and step left to a ledge. *Second Pitch:* Meander left about 45' (poorly protected though easy) and climb up to the base of the overhanging crack. *Third Pitch:* Follow the hand crack above to a ledge with 2 bolts. Rappel using 2 ropes.

95 *Variation I:* NO PAIN, NO GAIN
5.11D (not shown)

Fourth Pitch: Attack the vicious, overhanging finger crack above No Brain, No Pain. Belay from 2 bolts on a slab. *Fifth Pitch:* Romp up the low-angle face, then climb a short steep wall past a bolt to the top. Walk right to descend.

96 *Variation II*
5.7 (not shown)

The easiest way to approach No Pain, No Gain is to ascend right via a 50' traverse which begins near the top of Bits and Pieces. A 165' rope is required.

97 TEARS OF RAGE
II, 5.12A-A0; nuts to 2″ (not shown)

This climb is overhanging, thin, sustained, and desperate. The aid consists of a single hang on the crux pitch. *First Pitch:* Climb the first pitch of Bits and Pieces. *Second Pitch:* Follow the second pitch until it is possible to make an easy traverse right to a hanging belay. *Third Pitch:* Climb the crack (crux) and make a hard exit-move left at the top. Relatively easy face climbing leads up and right past a ledge and 2 bolts to the slab belay on No Pain, No Gain. *Fourth Pitch:* Climb the face above to the top.

98 BITS AND PIECES
I, 5.6; nuts to 2″, bolt protection

A fixed rappel has been established on Bits and Pieces and can be used to descend climbs topping out in the general vicinity. Two ropes are required for this rappel. Walk 100′ right on the west side of Asterisk Pass to a vertical water-polished groove. *First Pitch:* Follow the groove up and right to bolts directly under an overhang. *Second Pitch:* Skirt the overhang on the right and climb decomposed rock to the top.

99 SKYLIGHT
I, 5.10C; nuts to 2½″

Like No Brain, No Pain, the last pitch is marred by the first 2 pitches! However, it can be reached by climbing other routes in the area, and then downclimbing or rappelling Bits and Pieces a short distance to the beginning of the third pitch. Begin 50′ right of Asterisk Pass on the west side. *First Pitch:* Climb a series of slabs which lead up and right 80′ to a belay point with several fixed pins. *Second Pitch:* Continue up and right. Where the route intersects the Bits and Pieces gully, cut left and up to a belay ledge. *Third Pitch:* Traverse left 15′, and jam an overhanging hand crack above to the top.

100 SKY RIDGE
I, 5.8; nuts to 2″, bolt protection

Both the regular route and the variations are good climbs. Third class up the south side of Asterisk Pass to a roping-up spot. *First Pitch:* Climb straight up the west flank of the ridge to a good stance with bolts. *Second Pitch:* Step around to the east face. You'll be scared witless, but hand-traverse or foot-shuffle along a horizontal crack to solid ground.

101 *Variation I*
5.8

After climbing 40' on the first pitch, traverse right to a crack on the west face. Follow the crack until it joins the regular route on the crest of the ridge.

102 *Variation II:* SKYDIVER
5.10C

From the first belay, follow the crest of the ridge up and over an overhang to the top.

The Christian Brothers—West Side

The west side of the Christian Brothers can best be reached by climbing over Asterisk Pass.

103 THE AWL—INSIDE CORNER
I, 5.10C; nuts to 3/8"

A small spire (that's awl there is) on the west side of Asterisk Pass. It was first done free in 1961, a considerable achievement for that time in Oregon, or any place else for that matter. Pin scars have since made the climb *easier*. If you cannot do the climb cleanly, go climb dirty elsewhere.

104 CHRISTIAN BROTHERS TRAVERSE
III, 5.6

In the early sixties the Priest, the Monk, the Pope, the Friar, and the Abbot were climbed individually. Today, with the necessary bolts in place, all 5 summits can be done easily in a day. Sadly, the rock is not the best, but for those wishing to escape the rock gymnasium below, a trip through this seldom-traveled scenery is worthwhile. A small selection of nuts to 2½", a 3/8" bolt kit, and some slings for rappels are recommended. A south-to-north expedition is described below. A north-to-south excursion is possible. *First Pitch:* Start on the west side of the pinnacles, 100' from Asterisk Pass at a narrow chimney. Face climb outside of the chimney to a bolt belay. *Second Pitch:* Follow a ridge a short distance until good pocket holds on the east face lead to a chasm. Jump across and climb a slab to bolts. *Third Pitch:* Traverse left to a rotten crack, climb it for 10', then follow precarious holds to the summit of the Priest. *Fourth Pitch:* Rappel north into the Priest-Monk notch. *Fifth Pitch:* Traverse across the east face 10' to the summit chimney separating the twin summits of the Monk. Climb the chimney to the top. *Sixth Pitch:* From the summit of the Monk, rappel into a notch between Monk and Pope, a minor peak between Monk and

Friar. Belay on the Pope's summit. **Seventh Pitch:** Downclimb into a notch separating the Pope and the Friar. Ascend to the summit of the Friar. **Eighth Pitch:** Rappel into the amphitheater between the Friar and the Abbot. Boulder out the north side onto the east side of the Abbot. **Ninth Pitch:** Ascend a bolt line on the Abbot's northeast corner or retreat to the Cinnamon Slab rappel.

105 FALLEN ANGEL

I, 5.10C; bolt protection

Begin at a small inside corner facing left on a small buttress between the Awl and Midriff Bulge. Face climb past bolts to the top. The most difficult moves are encountered at the very start of the climb. Walk off to the right to descend.

106 MIDRIFF BULGE

I, 5.9 or 5.10A; nuts to 2½″

Just past the Awl is an awesome-looking roof split by a crack. After climbing over the roof, climb the crack and the face above until easy ledges allow a descent to the left.

107 SNAKE

II, 5.9; nuts to 4½″

After crossing Asterisk Pass, head downriver (north), keeping high along the cliff. After passing the Abbot, a boulder resembling a snake's head should be apparent just uphill from the trail. Behind the boulder is an off width. **First Pitch:** Follow the off-width crack to a belay ledge. **Second Pitch:** Follow a second smaller crack to the top. An established rappel is set up to the north of Snake and can be used for other climbs in the vicinity.

108 *Variations I and II*

5.7

The first belay can be gained via face climbing or a jam crack, both of which start to the left of the regular start.

109 THE GOLDEN ROAD

I, 5.10D; bolt protection

Start below a yellow-orange face between Snake and Cling-On. Face climb past 3 bolts to an anchor. Rappel.

110 CLING-ON

I, 5.9; nuts to 3½″

Start to the left of Snake in a left-facing corner. Climb the corner and traverse right to Snake. Rappel or climb Snake.

111 STRUNG-OUT
I, 5.9; nuts to 3" (not shown)

Start on the north-facing wall of the same buttress as Snake. Climb an overhanging crack with 2 distinct roofs higher up.

112 ANGEL FLIGHT BUTTRESS
I, 5.8; nuts to 1½" (not shown)

After Snake, the cliff line recedes and the path begins to climb. Ahead is a rotund buttress with an obvious dogleg crack called Spiderman. Behind are 2 north-facing black lichen buttresses. Angel Flight Buttress is the lower buttress on the right. Start on the left side of the buttress. *First Pitch:* Face climb past a few bolts and a short crack. Easy climbing up the low-angle face leads to a belay ledge. *Second Pitch:* Face climb past a couple of bolts to the top.

113 HEAVEN CAN WAIT
I, 5.7 (not shown)

Start on the south face of Angel Flight Buttress at the bottom of a left-facing dihedral. *First Pitch:* Climb the dihedral to a ledge. *Second Pitch:* Move left on an easy unprotected face for 20', then climb straight up to a bolt on Angel Flight Buttress. Continue to the top.

114 HIGH SAGE
I, 5.9 or 5.10A; nuts to 2" (not shown)

A difficult climb to rate because the hardest moves are right off the ground. The upper portion of the climb is poorly protected. Begin at the low point of the upper or left-hand buttress. Face climb up to a bolt. Continue straight up until it is possible to walk off left.

Spiderman Buttress

The next formation after Angel Flight Buttress is a rotund cliff with an obvious dogleg crack.

115 TARANTULA
I, 5.11D; nuts to 2½"

Exceedingly awkward in places, though still a worthwhile climb with athletic moves and solid rock. An obvious roof crack on the right side of the Spiderman Buttress. *First Pitch:* Chimney the right side of a gigantic block to a large ledge. *Second Pitch:* Climb to the roof. Undercling left to a bolt, then struggle 15' up an overhanging finger crack past another bolt. Easier climbing leads to a bolt belay on top.

116 SPIDERMAN

I, 5.7; nuts to 2½″

There are 2 starts to Spiderman: a left-facing dihedral on the left or a crack breaking a slab on the right. *First Pitch:* Climb either start to a dogleg crack. Belay above the dogleg on a sloping ledge. *Second Pitch:* Escape left or climb up and right around a large roof to the top.

117 WIDOW MAKER

I, 5.9; nuts to 1¼″

Follow the left start of Spiderman for 30′. Traverse left to a flake crack and follow it to the top. Take many small and medium nuts, as the crack obstinately refuses to permit satisfying placements.

118 EXPLOSIVE ENERGY CHILD

I, 5.10C; nuts to ¼″, bolt protection

Start left of Spiderman at a small triangle formed by two converging dihedrals. Edge on explosive pebbles for 40′ to a crack. Continue up and left to a belay. Rappel or follow In Harm's Way to the top.

119 IN HARM'S WAY

I, 5.7; nuts to 1″, bolt protection

Start to the left of Spiderman. Climb to a ledge below a black lichen-covered face using either of 2 cracks. Nip up nubbins to a bolt belay. Traverse right to ramps leading topside.

120 LITTLE FEAT

I, 5.10B; nuts to 2½″

Start below a large right-facing dihedral on Spiderman Buttress. Climb to a ledge system 40′ up. Follow the corner to an alcove below the top. Finish up an obvious hand crack (5.10B) or scramble straight up. An intricate crux on fine rock that is spoiled somewhat by rotten rock in the section below.

121 DR. DOOM

I, 5.9; nuts to 6″ (not shown)

Awkward, strenuous, and poorly protected. Start on the right side of a large pillar on the north side of Spiderman Buttress. *First Pitch:* Climb the right side of the pillar using an off width. *Second Pitch:* From the top of the pillar, climb a second off width to the top.

122 NECROMANCER

I, 5.8; nuts to 2″ (not shown)

Climb the left-hand crack of 2 parallel cracks on the north side of Spiderman Buttress.

Opposite, Mesa Verde Wall and Spiderman Buttress from the west (Alan Kearney photo)

Mesa Verde Wall

To the north of Spiderman Buttress is a large formation called Mesa Verde Wall.

123 CAPTAIN FINGERS
I, 5.10A; nuts to 1″

A thin crack on the right side of Mesa Verde Wall. See the photograph for the exact location.

124 WESTERN CHIMNEYS
I, 5.5

Climb up to and behind the large tower formation on the right side of Mesa Verde Wall. Exit right near the top of the tower.

125 PALO VERDE
III, 5.4-A3 or A4; nuts and pins to 1½″

A thin crack system in the center of Mesa Verde Wall. *First Pitch:* Scramble up easy rock to the base of the wall. *Second Pitch:* Twenty feet of easy free climbing starts the remaining 100′ of aid. Belay above a large roof at bolts. *Third Pitch:* Continue straight up the crack system, through questionable rock, to a juniper tree belay at the top.

126 AND 127 UNNAMED CRACKS

Two unnamed cracks lead to a ledge system on the lower half of Mesa Verde Wall. From right to left as they appear in the photo, they are graded I, 5.7 and I, 5.8.

128 CHIMNEY DE CHELLY
II, 5.10A; nuts to 2″

Start in a right-facing dihedral on the west face of Mesa Verde Wall. *First Pitch:* Climb the dihedral until it is possible to traverse right into potholes. At the top of the potholes, a hard move to the right ends on a belay ledge. *Second Pitch:* Face climbing leads up to the base of a large chimney. *Third Pitch:* Climb a chimney to the top. Descend down easy ledges on the north side of Mesa Verde Wall.

129 *Variation:* DESOLATION ROW
5.10D

Rather than traversing out of the dihedral on the first pitch, continue to a triangular roof. Zip over the roof past a bolt to a ledge. Easy climbing leads to the second belay on Chimney De Chelly.

130 TALE OF TWO S#@%&

II, 5.10A; nuts to 2"

Begin below a crack between Minas Morgul and Chimney De Chelly. *First Pitch:* Follow several crack systems to a steep ramp. *Second Pitch:* Climb an overhanging right-leaning crack to a good belay on a pedestal. *Third Pitch:* Follow a short corner to face climbing above. Belay at a large ledge. Descend down easy ledges on the north side of Mesa Verde Wall.

131 DOWN SYNDROME

I, 5.10A; nuts to 1½", bolt protection

Climb a short dihedral between Minas Morgul and Tale of Two S#@%&. From the top of the dihedral, face climb up 30' past 3 bolts, and traverse left 10' to Minas Morgul. Rappel. Good crack and face climbing on excellent rock.

132 MINAS MORGUL

II, 5.11D; nuts to 2"

Start at a 30' block leaning against the northwest face of Mesa Verde Wall. *First Pitch:* Climb a chimney between the block and the main wall, then continue on some bad rock to a hanging belay. *Second Pitch:* Climb a thin finger crack splitting an overhanging wall. Clear a roof above (crux) and belay at 3 bolts. *Third Pitch:* Climb a low-angle crack on good rock past a small roof, then finish up a steep finger crack. Descend down easy ledges on the north side of Mesa Verde Wall.

133 *Variation*

5.8

A more enjoyable start face climbs past 2 bolts up a 30' block at the beginning of the route.

134 TREZLAR

I, 5.10A; nuts to 2½" (not shown)

Climb an exhilarating, clean left-facing corner on the north side of Mesa Verde Wall. As an aid climb, Trezlar was called Raindance. Descend down easy ledges on the left.

135 LICHENS PERSUASION

I, 5.7; nuts to 2" (not shown)

There are 2 corners left of Trezlar. Lichens Persuasion follows the one farthest left. Descend down easy ledges on the left.

Monkey Face

Monkey Face is a spectacular 400' spire which, when seen from the south, forms the features of a grinning simian. The best approach is via Asterisk Pass.

The descent from Monkey Face involves 3 rappels off the east side. Bolts at the summit provide a short rappel to the Nose Cave. The Nose is a large boulder with bolts on its "exposed" side. These bolts allow a 140' rappel (two ropes are mandatory) to easy ledges on the east side just below the Notch separating the parent cliff from Monkey Face. From here, climb down easy ledges or make one more short rappel to the ground.

136 DIAMONDS AND RUST
II, 5.8; nuts to 2" (not shown)

Diamonds and Rust follows the buttress immediately south of the west face of Monkey Face. Begin on the left side of the buttress, under an overhang. Clear the overhang on the right and follow the ridge crest for 4 pitches to the top. Beware of very poor rock in several places.

137 PERPETUAL MOTION
I, 5.9; nuts to 2"

Start on the southern side of Monkey Face's west wall at the base of an impressive arch capped by a roof. Traverse left 15' on miserable rock to the arch. Race up to an anchor and rappel.

138 DOLF'S DIHEDRAL
I, 5.9; nuts to 2"

This is a short right-leaning crack left and parallel with the lower part of Perpetual Motion. Start as for Perpetual Motion and continue traversing left to a ledge at the base of the dihedral. Jam to a belay spot. Rappel. One of Smith Rock's finest hand cracks—all 25' of it.

139 POTENTIAL ENERGY
II, 5.10B; nuts to 4"

Immediately left of the start of Perpetual Motion is an obvious left-leaning flake crack. *First Pitch:* Layback up the flake past a bulge and continue to a ledge. Follow Dolf's Dihedral for 15', then move left via a tricky mantle to a large ledge. Belay at bolts on the left. *Second Pitch:* Scamper up the face on so-so rock. After a difficult move (crux) on good rock, face climb 35' to a ledge. *Third Pitch:* Ramble up and right on easy, low-angle ramps for about 40'. Pull over several small roofs to the top. Walk right to descend. A respectable route with varied climbing.

Protection is somewhat difficult in places though the crux moves are well protected.

140 *Variation*

A3

The original start followed a seam just left of a large juniper tree at the base of the wall.

141 KING KONG

II, 5.9; nuts to 4"

Start at the base of a ramp leading to a left-facing corner in the middle of the west face of Monkey Face. *First Pitch:* Climb up and right and follow a crack through a small bulge above. Belay in an alcove. *Second Pitch:* Traverse across a steep face about 10' to the base of a crack. Belay. *Third Pitch:* Follow the crack and from the top traverse left to the West Face Variation belay stance. *Fourth Pitch:* Climb to the top of the cliff or traverse to the Notch.

142 *Variation I*

5.10A

On the ground start 20' to the right of the ramp. Climb directly up to the crack on the third pitch of the regular route.

143 *Variation II*

5.8

Halfway up the crack on the third pitch, follow a crack up and left until rejoining the route.

144 GODZILLA

II, 5.8; nuts to 3"

First Pitch: Climb the first pitch of King Kong. *Second Pitch:* Continue up a crack above and clear an overhang near its top. Move left to the West Face Variation belay. *Third Pitch:* Climb to the top of the cliff or traverse to the Notch.

145 SMAUG

II, 5.10B; nuts to 2½"

Start as for King Kong. *First Pitch:* Follow a crack and dihedral system directly above the ramp leading to King Kong. When holds run out in the dihedral system, follow potholes up and left to a ledge. Belay behind a large boulder. *Second Pitch:* Climb a right-facing corner above to the West Face Variation. *Third Pitch:* Climb to the top of the cliff or traverse to the Notch.

146 MONKEY FARCE

I, 5.10B; nuts to 1″

Start just to the right of the West Face Variation. *First Pitch:* Follow a short overhanging crack onto a face. Face climb up and left to the first belay on the Southwest Corner. *Second Pitch:* Face climb horizontally left to the first belay on the West Face. Rappel.

147 WEST FACE VARIATION

II, 5.8; nuts to 2″

Begin at the base of a left-facing corner capped by a large block, or begin to the right in a left-slanting crack. Both starts lead to a ledge 30′ off the ground. *First Pitch:* Climb to the ledge. Follow a left-facing dihedral ramp system to an overhang. Move left and up around the overhang, clearing a block in the process. Work up a groove to a bolt belay. *Second Pitch:* Climb up a low-angle chimney until forced to move up and right. Gain the ramp above and traverse left 10′ to a belay. Rope drag is impossible to avoid unless you free solo this pitch. *Third Pitch:* Either climb up a chimney leading to the top of the parent cliff, or do some tricky moves onto an exposed but easy traverse to the Notch.

148 *Variation I*

5.8

From the first belay, traverse up and left 20′ to a hand/finger crack which leads to the Notch.

149 *Variation II*

5.8

Instead of traversing right on the second pitch, storm the overhang straight-on. Poor protection.

150 SOUTHWEST CORNER (with aid)

III, 5.6-C4; triple set of nuts ⅛″ to ⅜″, double set of nuts ½″ to 1½″, 2 cliffhangers, small tie-off loops. ASTRO MONKEY (free climb), III, 5.11C; double set of nuts ⅛″ to 1½″

An excellent route with or without aid. Begin midway between the West Face Variation and the West Face in a right-slanting crack capped by an overhang. *First Pitch:* Climb the crack (5.11C or C4) 140′ to a belay. *Second Pitch:* Climb a short steep finger crack. Easier climbing leads up a ramp to a belay beneath an overhanging corner. *Third Pitch:* Wild climbing (5.11A or C3) leads to the Southwest Corner. Mantle onto a ledge under a second overhang. *Fourth Pitch:* Swing

Monkey Face from the west (Don Lowe photo)

out and clear the overhang. Follow a crack to Bohn Street. *Fifth Pitch:* Climb the Pioneer Route, West Face Cave, Monkey Space, or rappel off.

151 *Variation I*
5.7

To gain the first belay on Southwest Corner without difficulty, climb the first pitch of the West Face Variation and belay. Traverse left 40' to the belay bolts on Southwest Corner.

152 *Variation II*
5.5

If it is getting late, step right from the second belay and climb an overhanging chimney. Traverse to the Notch and escape down the east-side ledges.

153 *Variation III*
5.11A

At a resting point on the third pitch, move right via a horizontal crack and climb up to the Notch.

154 WEST FACE
III, 5.7-C3; nuts to 1½", mostly ⅛" to 1"

Begin at the extreme left edge of the west face of Monkey Face. *First Pitch:* Mixed free and aid leads up a crack 140' to a belay ledge. *Second, Third and Fourth Pitches:* Bolt ladders lead to the top. The first pitch has gone free from the fourth bolt on at 5.12B. The fourth pitch goes free at 5.11B.

155 NORTHWEST PASSAGE
III, 5.7-C3; or III, 5.12B-C3; nuts to 1½", mostly ⅛" to 1" (not shown)

First Pitch: Climb the first pitch of the West Face (5.7, C3 or 5.12B-A0). *Second Pitch:* Move up and around the northwest corner and follow a thin crack to a hanging belay (C3 or 5.11C). *Third Pitch:* Climb the North Face crack to the West Face Cave (C3). *Fourth Pitch:* Follow a bolt line out the northwest end of the Cave to the summit (C1 or 5.11B). Exhilarating climbing whether on aid or free.

156 *Variation*
5.8 (not shown)

Avoid the first pitch by gaining ledges on the north face. Traverse horizontally to the northwest corner to join the regular route.

157 NORTH FACE

III, 5.5-C3; nuts to 1½″, mostly ⅛″ to ½″ (not shown)

The new wire nuts make an all-nut ascent easier and safer than before. Scramble to the base of the climb via ledges on the northeast corner. *First Pitch:* Aid up a bolt ladder and follow a crack (C2 or 5.10D) to a bolt belay. *Second Pitch:* Continue in the crack. Free climb up and right just before the West Face Cave. *Third Pitch:* Follow a bolt line out the northwest end of the Cave to the summit (C1 or 5.11B).

158 EAST FACE

III, 5.7-A3 or C4; nuts to 2″, mostly ⅛″ to 1″ (not shown)

Climb up easy ledges on the east side to the base of a long thin overhanging crack. *First Pitch:* Aid leads up about 90′ to a bolt belay. *Second Pitch:* Spectacular aid leads to a traverse and a bolt line. Belay above on a ledge. *Third Pitch:* Bolts lead over an overhang to face climbing and the top. To do the route clean, take 10 nuts size ⅜″, for the first pitch and numerous small wire nuts.

159 RISING EXPECTATIONS

I, 5.12A; nuts to 2″, mostly ¼″ to 1″ (not shown)

Gain access to the climb via ledges on the east side of Monkey Face. Start below an overhanging thin crack just right of a corner leading to the Notch between the parent cliff and Monkey Face. Climb the thin crack to Bohn Street. Rappel. If the start doesn't finish you, the finish probably will.

160 PIONEER ROUTE

II, 5.7-C1; nuts 1″ to 2½″, 40 carabiners

Gain access to the Notch between the parent cliff and Monkey Face via ledges on the east side. Although relatively simple, a rope may be needed for the first few feet. *First Pitch:* Climb to the Notch, follow a crack, face climb past a bolt, and belay on a conspicuous south-facing ledge called Bohn Street. *Second Pitch:* Climb the Chrome Moly Bolt line to the Mouth Cave. *Third Pitch:* Free (5.7) or aid out the eastern side of the Cave (often called Panic Point), to a sizable boulder and 3 bolts. (These bolts are the beginning of the 140′ rappel for descent.) Traverse right around the boulder to the Nose Cave. *Fourth Pitch:* Easy (5.1) climbing leads to the top.

161 BOHN STREET WEST FACE CAVE

II, 5.6-A3; nuts and pins to 1½″

First Pitch: Climb the first pitch of the Pioneer Route. *Second Pitch:* Climb a crack to the left of the bolt line, which leads to the West Face

Cave. *Third Pitch:* Follow a bolt line out the northwest end of the Cave to the summit (C1 or 5.11B).

162 MONKEY SPACE
II, 5.11B; nuts to 1″, bolt protection

Excellent rock, excellent protection, and excellent climbing combine to provide one of the best climbs at Smith Rock. *First Pitch:* Climb the first pitch of the Pioneer Route. *Second Pitch:* Traverse up and left from the left end of Bohn Street. Climb up and over a bulge, then follow a crack up and right to the West Face Cave. *Third Pitch:* Climb out the ceiling on the northwest end of the West Face Cave to the top.

Fairy Tale Tower

Just to the north of Monkey Face is a large gully. Fairy Tale Tower is a buttress located at the very top of the gully.

163 THE MADCAP ADVENTURES OF MR. TOAD
I, 5.8 (not shown)

"Mr. Toad" climbs the clean face in the center of Fairy Tale Tower in 2 pitches. Descend off the back side.

164 CHICKEN LITTLE
I, 5.5 (not shown)

Chicken Little follows a left-facing corner on the left side of the buttress. Two pitches are required to get to the top. Descend off the back side.

Kiss of the Leper Buttress

The formation immediately north of Monkey Face is called Kiss of the Leper Buttress.

165 GREAT EXPECTATIONS
I, 5.7; nuts to 2½″ (not shown)

Climb a clean open book approximately halfway up the gully face of Kiss of the Leper Buttress.

166 SCABBIES
I, 5.7 (not shown)

Walk past a large roof on the west face of the Buttress. A nondescript start leads to a ramp. Climb bathtub-sized potholes above to a ledge. Continue face climbing to the top. Not recommended because of extremely rotten rock.

New World Buttress

From Monkey Face hike downriver (north). The last major welded tuff formation on the right is called New World Buttress.

167 NEW WORLD
II, 5.8 (not shown)

Start on the left side of the buttress and climb to a crack. Follow the crack to the top. It's a long (5-pitch) route with sections of excellent rock and sections of terrible rock.

168 HAWKLINE MONSTER
II, 5.10A; nuts to 2½″ (not shown)

Rope up below the right-hand dihedral in the river face of New World Buttress. Follow the dihedral to the top (3 pitches with bolt belays). This route also has a mixture of good and bad rock and is not recommended.

Red Wall

Cross the Crooked River footbridge and follow a steep path up and right. After passing Picnic Lunch Wall and a deep narrow canyon, the path levels out at the base of Red Wall, one of the finest crags in Oregon. To descend from the top of Red Wall, walk west and then north to a long gully known as Misery Ridge. An established trail, not readily apparent from the top, leads down Misery Ridge to the base of Red Wall. Stay on this trail to minimize your impact on the already heavily scarred hillside.

169 BILL'S FLAKE
I, 5.10A; nuts to 3″

A small circular flake on the left side of Red Wall. Scramble to a ledge, then hand jam the left side of the flake. The rappel anchor at the top was poorly placed and had not been replaced by the time this book went to press.

170 PAPER TIGER
II, 5.10A; nuts to 2½″

When the rotten roof is cleared off, this will be a fine climb. Begin below Bill's Flake. *First Pitch:* Scramble to the base of Bill's Flake and move right 15′ behind a flake. *Second Pitch:* Climb a hand crack up and right to an alcove. A fixed pin protects a hard move left on rotten rock over the roof. A bolt belay can be found up and left in a small cave. *Third Pitch:* Climb left and up and right to a small ledge with sage brush. Move up and left to a two-bolt belay. *Fourth Pitch:* Move right and up across a slab and follow a crack to the top.

171 SUPER SLAB
II, 5.6; nuts to 2″
One of the better climbs at Smith Rock. After the trail levels out below the Red Wall, it passes a large shattered amphitheater. Rope up just left of the amphitheater at the base of a ramp. *First Pitch:* Climb the ramp to a wide belay ledge. *Second Pitch:* Traverse left using potholes to gain a stance below a second ramp. *Third Pitch:* Swarm up the second ramp to the cliff top. *Fourth Pitch:* Downclimb into a gully on the left and climb a slab to gain Misery Ridge, or rappel the route using 2 ropes.

172 *Variation I:* PANAMA EXPRESS
5.8
Climb about 15′ up the third pitch of Super Slab. Split right and follow a crack to the spot where it joins the final 20′ of Panama Red. Climb to the rim.

173 *Variation II:* PANAMA RED
5.8
Directly above the first belay on Super Slab, climb a steep slab past several bolts, which are not visible from below. Above, climb the right side of a large block to the top.

174 *Variation III:* AMPHETAMINE GRIP
5.7
Above the first belay on Super Slab, climb an overhanging dihedral to a small ledge. Face climb above until holds lead left to white rock. Climb a corner to the top. The top portion of "Grip" is unprotected but surprisingly many people enjoy it.

175 IRON CURTAIN
I, 5.9; nuts to 1″
Past Super Slab, the trail loses about 30′. Iron Curtain more or less follows a shallow inside corner facing left, which starts before the trail levels out again. Use 2 ropes to rappel from a ledge 100′ up.

176 HELTER SKELTER
II, 5.10C; nuts to 2½″
Poorly protected on the first and third pitches. Begin in a tiny crack 5′ to the right of Iron Curtain. *First Pitch:* Face climb to a bolt. Follow the crack 10′ until face holds lead up and left to a second bolt. Climb

straight up to the same belay ledge used for Iron Curtain. *Second Pitch:* Climb a shallow corner above the belay past several bolts (crux). Continue up the corner until progress is blocked by an overhang. *Third Pitch:* Traverse left 20' to 30', climb up 20' to 30', and traverse right and up. Belay at the first opportunity. *Fourth Pitch:* Climb a corner to the top.

177 *Variation I*

5.8

The first belay can be gained by traversing high from an alcove on the left.

178 *Variation II:* IF SIX WERE NINE

5.10A

Rather than climbing left on face holds on the first pitch, continue up and right in the thin crack to the first belay.

179 CHAIRMAN MAO'S LITTLE RED BOOK

I, 5.11A; nuts to ½"

Start in a left-facing corner, 15' right of Helter Skelter. Climb up the corner to a ledge. Belay. Continue up a right-facing corner above (crux) to the first belay on Helter Skelter. Rappel using 2 ropes.

180 FINGERS OF FATE

I, 5.10D; nuts to 1½"

First Pitch: Climb the first pitch of Chairman Mao's Little Red Book. *Second Pitch:* Move right and climb a right-facing corner to a ledge. Continue up a clean fingercrack which arches left over a small roof to a bolt. A strenuous boulder move (crux) finishes to a small ledge. Rappel using 2 ropes.

181 GONE WITH THE FLAKE

I, 5.9; nuts to 4"

Above a low point in the trail is a large flake with an overhanging left side. Climb the left side, treading carefully on loose flakes in the middle. Downclimb and rappel the right side of the flake to descend.

182 HO CHI MINH TRAIL

II, 5.7-A2

Ho Chi Minh Trail begins just to the right of Gone with the Flake in a section of broken rock. The upper half of the route follows a dihedral about 40' left of the upper half of Peking.

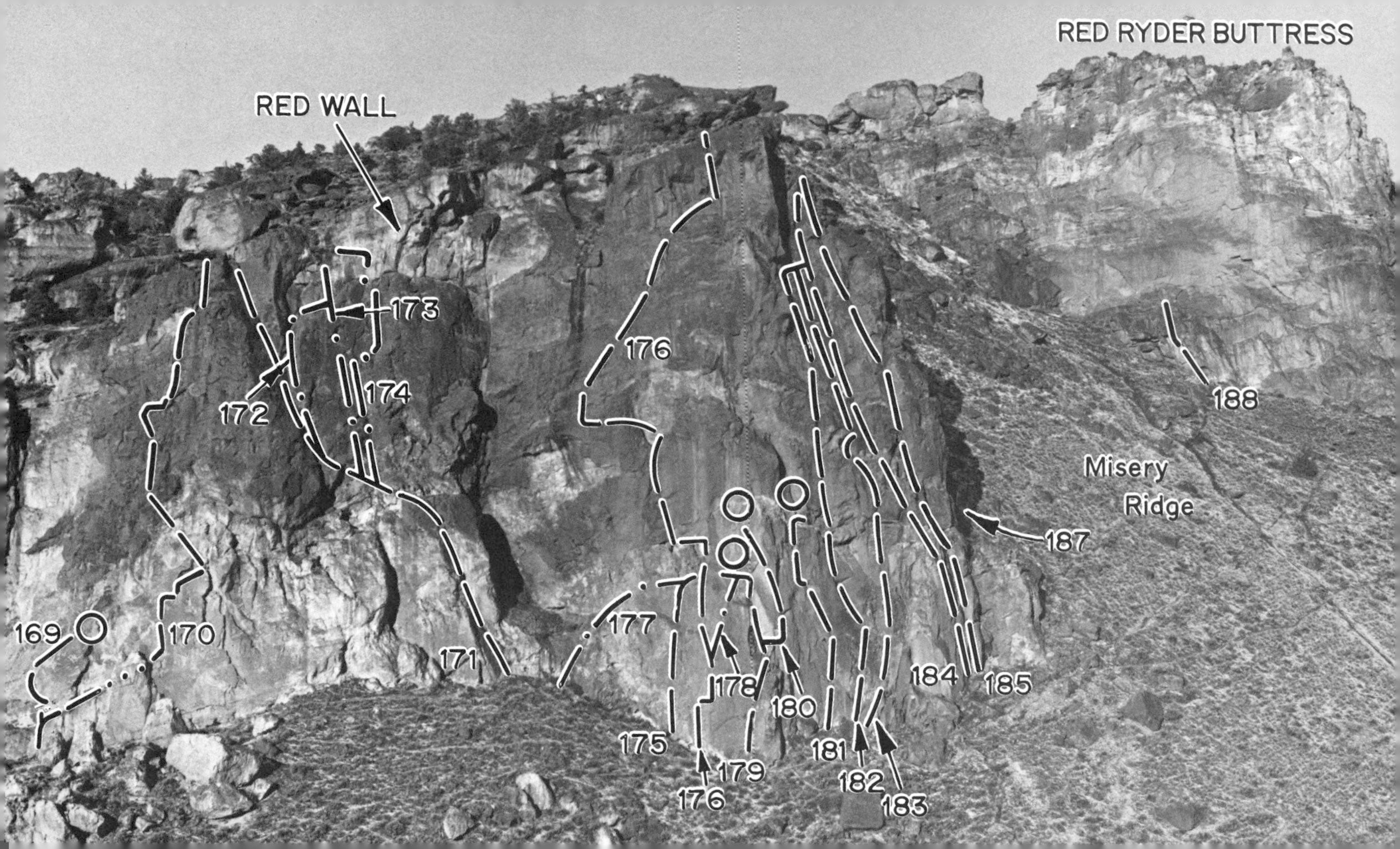

RED RYDER BUTTRESS

RED WALL

173

172

174

176

169 170

171

177

175

176

178

179

180

181

182

183

184

185

187

Misery
Ridge

188

183 SHANGHAI
II, 5.10A; nuts to 3″

Start as for Ho Chi Minh Trail. *First Pitch:* Climb easy cracks and slabs to a short overhanging hand crack. Jam the crack (crux) and follow a gully to a ledge. *Second Pitch:* Move left, then undercling a short right-leaning crack over a roof. Go left to a ledge. *Third Pitch:* Wander directly up the face above (poor protection) until it is possible to traverse into the upper part of Peking.

If the names of the following 2 climbs always elude you, remember that, ideologically, Peking is to the *left* of Moscow.

184 PEKING
II, 5.8; nuts to 1½″

On the right side of Red Wall are 2 parallel cracks which extend from the bottom of the cliff to its top. The left-hand crack is Peking.

185 MOSCOW
II, 5.6; nuts to 1¾″

On the right side of Red Wall are 2 parallel cracks which extend from the bottom of the cliff to its top. The right-hand crack is Moscow. On a good weekend, an alpine start is advisable to avoid the crowds.

186 *Variation:* MONGOLIANS
5.10A (not shown)

Begin 10′ to the left of Moscow. Climb a short, steep thin crack until it is possible to rejoin Moscow. The climb name honors the first ascent party and the intelligence it took to find and climb this ridiculous line.

187 HAVANA
I, 5.6; nuts to 2″ (not shown)

Climb discontinuous crack systems on the northeast face of Red Wall. The climb starts above, to the right of, and just around the corner from Moscow.

Red Ryder Buttress

A large forgettable buttress near the top of Misery Ridge.

188 I ALMOST DIED
I, 5.11A; nuts to 2″

After passing Red Wall, the Misery Ridge Trail begins its long uphill slog. After crossing to the right side of the gully, the trail passes a left-

Opposite, Red Wall and Red Ryder Buttress from the east (Jeff Thomas photo)

leaning corner capped by a roof. Climb the corner and the roof above to a ledge. Walk off left. I Almost Died is a testpiece for this grade of climbing at Smith Rock.

189 RED RYDER
I, 5.8; nuts to 1″, bolt protection

At the right side of the above-mentioned gully, continue right off the trail and around a line of boulders. Scramble up their right side to a ledge system at the base of a steep red face. *First Pitch:* On the left side of the face, climb past a thin crack to a bolt belay. *Second Pitch:* Climb up and left to a decomposing crack which leads to rappel bolts.

190 *Variation:* FLEX
5.9

Start 10′ to the left of Red Ryder. Climb a short low-angle thin crack to the first belay of Red Ryder.

191 THE YOUNG AND THE RESTLESS
I, 5.9; nuts to 1¾″, bolt protection

Start just to the right of Red Ryder. *First Pitch:* Ascend slab on the right of Red Ryder to an alcove belay. *Second Pitch:* Traverse left and up onto a ramp beneath a roof. Continue left on shaky flakes until able to clear the roof. Move left to belay bolts on Red Ryder. Rappel.

192 *Variation:* THE YOUNG AND THE WORTHLESS
5.7

From the first belay on The Young and the Restless, climb an obvious crack system above to the top of the cliff.

London Tower

Cross the Crooked River footbridge, turn right, and follow a level trail upriver (north). After the trail passes a large 80′ ponderosa pine and begins to curve right (northeast), London Tower can be seen on the left. It is distinguished by a large chimney/crack system in the upper third of its river face.

193 LONDON TOWER
II, 5.10A (not shown)

An exact description of the route is not available, but the crux is 15′ of face climbing which leads to the upper chimney/crack system. Not recommended because of rotten rock.

Red Ryder Buttress (Jeff Thomas photo)

Little Three Fingered Jack

Little Three Fingered Jack is the second rock point on the rim west of the Monument.

194 CHOCKSTONE CHIMNEY

I, 4 (not shown)

From the ridge behind Little Three Fingered Jack, drop down to the east side of the formation. Climb a chimney past a chockstone to the summit.

195 VICTORY OF PROLETARIAN PEOPLE'S AMBITION ARETE

III, 5.7 (not shown)

An exact description of the route is not available. All that is known is that the climb starts in the center of the river face of Little Three Fingered Jack.

The Monument

Follow the river trail from the Crooked River footbridge as it curves east. Lining the northern wall of the canyon are a series of rock towers. The northernmost and largest tower—the Monument—has an impressive southwest face.

196 NORTH RIDGE

I, 4 (not shown)

Scramble up either of 2 gullies which border the west and east sides of the Monument. Climb up the obvious north ridge behind the tower. Downclimb or rappel to descend.

197 ABRAXAS

IV, 5.7-C3 or III, 5.10D-A0; aid rack: triple set of nuts $^1/_8$″ to $^3/_8$″, double set of nuts ½″ to 1¼″, triple set of nuts 1½″ to 2″, 2 cliffhangers. Free rack: nuts to 1″, double set of nuts 1¼″ to 2″

Potholes, which are large enough to be bathtubs if they were turned upright, mark the base of the southwest face of the Monument. Rope up at their base. *First Pitch:* Diagonal up to the highest pothole on the right side. *Second Pitch:* Traverse right to a chimney. Tossing off loose rock as you go, climb up this rotten corridor to a hand traverse left to a bolt belay. *Third Pitch:* Aid (C3) or free (5.10D) up miserable discontinuous seams to a pedestal. *Fourth Pitch:* A very thin crack (C3 or 5.10D-A0) leads to an alcove just below a rotten band of rock. *Fifth*

Opposite, South side of the Monument and surrounding summits (Jeff Thomas photo)

SQUAW ROCK

LITTLE THREE FINGERED JACK

THE MONUMENT

OSA THATCHER'S NEEDLE

202

201

203
204

197

198

199

LONDON TOWER
(193)

Pitch: Move up and right to the base of a single crack splitting an overhanging face. Aid (C1) or free (5.10C) the entire crack, passing a small roof midway. *Sixth Pitch:* Finish up a large chimney on the left. The fifth pitch, known as Tombstone Wall, is perhaps the most spectacular pitch at Smith Rock. Many people avoid the lower pitches of the climb by hiking to the top and rappelling. Two ropes and 2 rappels are required.

198 SANDS OF TIME

IV, 5.7-A4; protection unknown

A route description is not available for this climb.

199 SOUTHEAST FACE

III, 5.7-A4 or A5; protection unknown

Perhaps THE worst route at Smith Rock.

Osa Thatcher's Needle

Osa Thatcher's Needle is a slender tower attached to an unnamed formation east of the Monument.

200 OSA THATCHER'S NEEDLE

I, 5.6; protection unknown (not shown)

Hike up a gully to the east of the Monument. Gain a notch between Osa Thatcher's Needle and the parent cliff. Climb to the top of the formation. Rappel.

201 BIRD DUNG CHIMNEY

I, 5.1; protection unknown

Hike partway up a gully on the east side of the Monument. Climb a large bird dung-filled chimney to the top. Walk off north. Not recommended.

202 DECEPTION CRACK

I, 5.10A; protection unknown

Hike partway up a gully on the east side of the Monument. Easy climbing leads to the base of a thin crack. Follow the thin crack until it widens to a chimney. Belay. Climb to the top of Osa Thatcher's Needle or scramble off.

203 STREET WALKER

I, 5.6 (not shown)

Walk up the third gully to the right of the Monument. Climb a left-leaning crack up and around a blind corner to the top in one pitch. Walk off. A worthless route.

204 BRAIN SALAD SURGERY

I, 5.10D; nuts to 6", double set of nuts 1¾" (not shown)

Walk up the third gully to the right of the Monument. Look for a crack on the overhanging left side. (You will recognize it when you see it.) The crux is an off width, so take a full selection of large chocks. To descend, walk off to the east.

Liberty Bell and Juniper Spire

After passing the Monument, the trail curves south along the river. On your right, between the river and trail, is the old climbers' camp. On the left is a mass of rock distinguished by a slender pillar called Juniper Spire. To the left of Juniper Spire is a formation called Liberty Bell.

205 JUNIPER GULLY

I, 5.6-A1; protection unknown (not shown)

Climb the ugly gully between Juniper Spire and Liberty Bell to a notch. Follow a short bolt ladder out of the notch to the top of Liberty Bell. Rappel.

206 NORTH SIDE

I, 5.2; protection unknown (not shown)

Start on the north side of Liberty Bell and follow a chimney to the top. Rappel.

207 THE EAR

I, 5.7; protection unknown (not shown)

Climb the ugly gully between Juniper Spire and Liberty Bell to a notch. Traverse around and under a large "ear" on Juniper Spire. Merge with the Rib Traverse and either walk off or climb to the top. A two-rope rappel leads to the ground from the top.

208 UNNAMED AID CLIMB

I, A4; protection unknown (not shown)

Begin below the south side of the Juniper Spire proper. Follow discontinuous seams up and around to the west face of the spire. Continue to the top. A two-rope rappel leads to the ground from the top.

209 JAMBOREE
I, 5.8; nuts to 1¾" (not shown)

Start on the south side of the formation below a crack formed by the juncture of Juniper Spire proper and the connecting rib. Follow the crack to the base of the summit block. Climb to the summit or traverse the rib to easy ground. A two-rope rappel leads to the ground from the top.

210 RIB TRAVERSE
I, 5.1; nuts to 1¾"

Start on the uphill side of Juniper Spire on a ridge which connects the hillside to the spire. Follow the ridge up and around several gendarmes to the top of the summit block. A two-rope rappel leads to the ground from the top.

Staender Ridge

From the old climbers' camp, follow a trail uphill to an access road and irrigation canal. The irrigation canal disappears north into a tunnel, while the access road, known as the Burma Road, switchbacks up the hillside above. Between the top of the Burma Road and the irrigation tunnel is a succession of spires commonly called Staender Ridge. From a point where the Burma Road starts its uphill grind, begin hiking up a trail which leads to all the summits.

Most of the climbs on Staender Ridge are short and do not require lengthy explanation. The large number of easier climbs, combined with the brevity of the routes, should recommend the area to the neophyte. For more experienced climbers, Staender Ridge has good rock and several hard classics, so don't let the hike discourage you.

Starting with the first pinnacle fronting the irrigation canal, the named pinnacles are: Adit Rock, Control Tower, Independence Tower, the Mole, Bette's Needles, Flattop, and Staender Summit.

Adit Rock

This is the first pinnacle fronting the irrigation canal.

211 INSTANT REPLAY
I, 5.6; nuts to 2" (not shown)

There are 2 cracks on the south face of Adit Rock. Instant Replay follows the left crack.

Staender Ridge—
West Side
(Shari Nelson
photo)

212 PARKING LOT CRACK
I, 5.8; nuts to 6″ (not shown)

Parking Lot Crack follows the right crack. Near the top of the crack, either grunt up an off width or escape to the right on a ramp.

Control Tower

The next pinnacle is concealed except when seen from the west. Walk around the west side of Adit Rock past several large boulders to reach the base of Control Tower.

213 OUT-OF-CONTROL
I, 5.10C; nuts to 1¾″

Breaking the west wall of Control Tower is a thin face crack with an obscure and rotten start. Climb the crack to the top.

Independence Tower

By-pass Adit Rock on the east and follow the trail to the next spire, called Independence Tower.

214 MIDNIGHT RIDER
I, 5.10A; nuts to 1″

Start just left of the southeast corner. Climb face holds to a large ledge. A boulder move off the ledge (crux) on rotten rock leads to a crack which is climbed to the top.

215 FREE SPIRIT
I, 5.8; nuts to 1¾″

A narrow gully separates Independence Tower from a small pinnacle, just downhill, called Control Tower. At the west end of this gully is a thin crack which leads to the top.

216 D.A.R. (Daughters of the American Revolution) CRACK
I, 5.9; nuts to 4″

A large (you absolutely cannot miss it) liberated dihedral on the west side of Independence Tower.

217 NORTH SIDE
I, 5.1; nuts to 1″

A short dihedral which begins in the uphill notch between Independence Tower and the Mole. After the dihedral, climb a crack up and left to the summit.

The Mole

Immediately above Independence Tower is the Mole.

218 SLOPPER
I, 5.9; nuts to 1½"

A very short arching crack in a corner immediately right of Chopper.

219 CHOPPER
I, 5.8; nuts to 2"

Chopper is an open book on the east side of the Mole. The open book is partially formed by a large block which appears to have nothing important holding it in place.

220 SUNJAMMER
I, 5.10B; nuts to 1½"

A large overhanging open book on the southwest side of the Mole. Gain access to this climb by starting on the east side and scrambling through a col between Independence Tower and the Mole.

Bette's Needles

After the Mole, the next formation is Bette's Needles, with its large south face.

221 THRASHER
I, 5.8-A2; nuts to 2½"

Start on the southern face of Bette's Needles in a right-facing open book. Several moves of aid lead to an off width. At the top of the off width, scramble to the summit.

222 EASY STREET
I, 5.7; nuts to 2"

Start on the southernmost ridge of Bette's Needles. Circle around to the west face after one or two hard moves, and climb a chimney. A ridiculous line.

223 JUNIPER SNAG
I, 5.6; nuts to 1½"

From a juniper snag halfway down the western base of the Needles, climb directly into a chimney, then to the top.

INDEPENDENCE
TOWER

THE MOLE

BETTE'S
NEEDLES

STAENDER SUMMIT

FLATTOP

214

217

219

218

222

221

228

227

226

225

224 LIMESTONE CHIMNEY

I, 5.4; nuts to 2″

Start uphill in a col between Bette's Needles and the next formation above. Follow one of several easy and obvious routes to the top.

Flattop

Flattop is a square chunk of rock adjacent to Bette's Needles. It is distinguished by a summit block on its northern (uphill) end. The first 4 of the following 8 routes start on the east side of the rock, while the second 4 begin on the west side.

225 BUMP AND GRIND

I, 5.7; nuts to 2½″

Climb a right-facing corner on the uphill end of Flattop's east face. From the top of the open book, a 5.9 boulder move leads to the base of the summit block. Boulder to the top of the summit block.

226 LOST FOX

I, 5.8; nuts to 1¾″

Rope up below a buttress leading to the highest point of Flattop. Follow a crack splitting the buttress. From the top of the buttress, a 5.9 boulder move leads to the base of the summit block. Boulder to the top of the summit block.

227 SKID ROW

I, 5.6; nuts to 2″

Lurch up a left-facing corner just right of the east chimney route. Be wary of loose derelict rocks which line the route like so many drunks ready to fall. Boulder to the top of the summit block.

228 EAST CHIMNEY

I, 5.1; protection unknown

From the southeast side of the shoulder buttress at the downhill end of Flattop, climb an obvious zigzag ledge system to the entrance of the south chimney. Boulder to the top of the summit block.

229 SOUTH BUTTRESS

I, 5.1; protection unknown

Scramble up a sloping ledge on the west side of an adjoining buttress and follow it to where it levels out. Climb straight up the south end of the buttress to the top. Boulder to the top of the summit block.

Opposite, Staender Ridge—East Side (Alan Kearney photo)

230 LOWER WEST CHIMNEY
I, 5.1; protection unknown (not shown)

Stem a deep chimney on the lower west face. Boulder to the top of the summit block.

231 LIEBACK FLAKE
I, 5.4; protection unknown (not shown)

Climb a crack 20' left of the Lower West Chimney.

232 DIRECT NORTHWEST CRACK
I, 5.4 (not shown)

Climb a crack 30' left of the Lower West Chimney.

233 DELIVERANCE
I, 5.9 (not shown)

On the north side of Flattop, follow a crack to a ledge. Hard face climbing then leads to the top. To the author's knowledge, this climb has never been led.

Staender Summit

The last formation in the chain of summits is called Staender Summit.

234 SMUT
I, 5.12D; nuts to 2"

On the downhill side of Staender Summit is a 15' roof. Climb a thin finger crack which splits the roof (crux). Contine up a jam crack above to the summit. Whether you call it a climb or an elevated boulder problem, Smut has some of the most difficult roped moves at Smith Rock.

235 FALLING ROCK ZONE
I, 5.6; nuts to 2"

On the downhill side of Staender Summit is a 15' roof. Falling Rock Zone climbs a chimney just to the left of this roof. As the name implies, the rock is rotten.

236 NORTHWEST CORNER
I, 5.1; nuts to 2" (not shown)

Begin the climb at the northwest corner, taking an obvious route to a ledge. Continue straight up the northwest corner via a vertical jam crack.

237 DESIDERATA

I, 5.9; nuts to 1" (not shown)

Desiderata is a large left-facing corner on the east side of Staender Summit. The climbing involves a thin finger crack and stemming up a perfect 90 degree corner, with a short off-width move at the top. Well worth the hike.

238 DEFECATION CRACK

I, 5.7; nuts to 1¾" (not shown)

Climb a short off width in the middle of the east face of Staender Summit to a ramp. Follow the ramp to the summit.

239 PEANUTS

I, 5.7; nuts to 2½" (not shown)

On the downhill side of the east face of Staender Summit, climb a chimney which leads to a left-facing open book. Climb to the summit.

French Tent Rock

The highest spire east of the Monument and west of Staender Summit. The original name, French Tent Rock, is used in place of No Name, a misnomer used for the past 15 years.

240 SOUTH BOWL

I, 5.1; protection unknown (not shown)

From the southern bowl, climb to a notch. Follow the west ridge to the top.

241 NORTH LEDGE

I, 5.6; protection unknown (not shown)

On the north side of the formation, climb to a ledge and follow a short left-facing corner above to the spot where it joins the west ridge. Follow the ridge to the summit.

Rotten Crack

Halfway up the hillside between Staender Ridge and the Burma Road is a small isolated pinnacle called Rotten Crack.

242 ROTTEN CRACK

I, 5.8; protection unknown (not shown)

Start in a small dihedral on the west side of the formation. Follow the dihedral to the top. Only those desperate for something new will wish to try this climb.

243 FRICTION ARETE

I, 5.1; protection unknown (not shown)

To climb this route, follow the ridge on the downhill side of Rotten Crack. The rock is rotten and protection is difficult to find.

The Dinosaur

The Dinosaur is a large formation just to the left of Burma Road at its high point. It is split into 2 parts. The southern segment, or downhill side, is a slab. The uphill segment is a pinnacle.

244 ORANGE PEEL

I, 5.6; bolt protection (not shown)

Orange Peel begins downhill from a juniper tree on the west side of the downhill slab.

245 LEMON PEEL

I, 5.8; bolt protection (not shown)

Lemon Peel begins uphill from a juniper tree on the west side of the downhill slab.

246 COW PIE

I, 5.7; protection unknown (not shown)

Cow Pie follows a chimney with no protection on the south face of the uphill pinnacle.

Marsupial Crags

Looking southeast from the base of Burma Road, the observant will see a series of rock spires. The largest and highest rock is the Wombat, followed by Opossum, Tail, Brogan Spire, and Mini Half Dome. On the south side of Mini Half Dome, near the irrigation canal, are Kangaroo, Joey, and Wallaby. On the north side of Mini Half Dome is a small spire called Delirium Tremens. Finally, just above a switchback in the Burma Road, is Koala Rock.

Koala Rock

Walk up the Burma Road. At the turnout where the Burma Road switchbacks, leave the road and hike up to Koala Rock.

247 THIN AIR

I, 5.8; nuts to 1¾″

The lowest point on Koala Rock is a buttress forming the right edge of

Opposite, Marsupial Crags (Shari Nelson photo)

the west face. On the west face of this buttress, climb face holds and a gradually widening crack over an overhang. Downclimb ledges on the left to descend. A good climb.

248 CATTY CORNER
I, 5.8; nuts to 3″

To the left of Thin Air is a left-facing dihedral with 2 cracks. Climb the crack on the right, the difficulty of which will vary according to hand size. Downclimb ledges on the left to descend.

249 CRAZIES
I, 5.7; nuts to 2″

Climb a crack just to the left of Catty Corner, avoiding a killer flake halfway up. Downclimb ledges on the left to descend.

250 DESERT SOLITAIRE
I, 5.9; nuts to 1½″, bolt protection

Fourth class up to a large ledge in the center of the rock's west face. *First Pitch:* From the left edge of the ledge, gorilla over several overhangs to the base of a left-facing corner. *Second Pitch:* Climb a corner to the top.

251 ROUND RIVER
I, 5.1; nuts to 2″, bolt protection

Round River starts on the left edge of the west face, beside a juniper tree. The route follows low-angle slabs, eventually swinging onto the north face. An excellent route for beginners if you are up for the hike.

252 *Variation*
5.8

Instead of traversing onto Koala's north side, push straight up the northwest corner. Difficult to protect.

The Wombat

From Koala Rock, hike uphill to a massive rock called the Wombat.

253 CATFIGHT CRACKS
II, 5.9; nuts to 2½″

The second pitch is essentially a free solo for the leader; the climb is not recommended. Start just below the obvious thumb at the top of the southwest end of the Wombat. *First Pitch:* Follow a crack 100' to a bolt belay. *Second Pitch:* Switch right into a second crack and climb it to a belay stance. *Third Pitch:* Traverse right onto the south face of the Wombat and up to the Thumb notch.

254 C.L. CONCERTO
III, 5.9-A4; protection unknown

Start in a short overhanging crack, about one-third of the way up the base of the west face of the Wombat. *First Pitch:* Climb the overhanging crack and scramble to a high point on easy ledges. *Second Pitch:* Aid climb up poor cracks to bolts and a hanging belay. *Third Pitch:* Difficult nailing leads up and left. *Fourth Pitch:* More aid leads further left to the top. A gross and ugly climb.

255 GREEN GULLY
I, 5.5; nuts to 1¼"

Scramble into a large gully halfway up the base of the west side of the Wombat. Easy but highly unaesthetic scrambling leads to a short roped pitch and the top.

256 WHITECLOUD
I, 5.7; nuts to 2"

If it is a nice day and the Dihedrals is crowded, grab a bite to eat and stroll over (and up) to this fine climb. The route follows a dihedral downhill from the left skyline on the west face. The bottom of the first pitch is difficult to protect, but the second pitch is fine crack climbing.

257 THE THUMB
II, 5.1; protection unknown

At the southern end of the Wombat is a formation resembling a thumb. Scramble along the top of the Wombat from its extreme northern end until a small 10' cliff is encountered. Either rappel or downclimb this cliff into a notch between it and the Thumb. After climbing the Thumb, climb out of the notch using a fixed rope or by some moderate (5.7) climbing.

Opossum, Tail, and Brogan Spire Complex
North Side

From Koala Rock, hike up to a pass between the Wombat and the next formation to the west. From east to west, the pinnacles on the formation are Opossum, Tail, and Brogan Spire.

258 DIAGONAL CRACK

I, 5.1; protection unknown (not shown)

On the east side of Opossum, follow the obvious diagonal crack that starts at the left side of the face and runs to the summit.

259 DOGFIGHT CRACK

I, 5.8; nuts to 2½" (not shown)

Rope up at the northeast corner of Opossum, just downhill from Diagonal Crack. Climb a crack with very rotten rock to the top.

260 TAIL

I, 5.1; protection unknown (not shown)

To climb the Tail, rappel or climb from the summit of Opossum.

261 THE GREAT ROOF

II, 5.4-C3; nuts to 1¼", mostly to ½"

A good aid climb if you do not mind overbolting and a blasted-out crack. Below Brogan Spire, on its north face, is a gargantuan roof with a thin crack breaking the face below it. *First Pitch:* Aid up the thin crack to a bolt belay. *Second Pitch:* Bolts lead out the roof to easy ground and a bolt belay. *Third Pitch:* Scramble to the top. To descend, return to the bolt belay at the end of the second pitch and rappel using two ropes.

262 PIN BENDER

II, 5.8-A2; protection unknown

Begin about 150' to the right of the Great Roof at the base of a crack. *First Pitch:* A short section of free climbing leads to aid in a dihedral and a bolt belay. *Second Pitch:* Hard free climbing leads to easy climbing and the top. *Third Pitch:* Use the Great Roof rappel to descend.

263 MINI HALF DOME

I, 5.8; bolt protection

Scramble to a notch between Brogan Spire and the next formation to the west, a miniature version of Half Dome. Move up a ramp onto the south face of Mini Half Dome, and make a few choice moves to the summit.

264 DELIRIUM TREMENS
I, 5.10A; nuts to 1¾"

Delirium Tremens is a small crag above the canal which sits just left (north) of the base of a ridge extending down from Mini Half Dome. On the northern side is an overhanging, right-facing open book. The name aptly describes the condition of any leader as he or she finishes, or tries to finish, the last few moves. An excellent climb with excellent rock.

Kangaroo, Joey, and Wallaby

The Kangaroo is the largest of the three formations just south of the Brogan complex and close to the irrigation canal. The formation connected to the Kangaroo by a notch is called Joey. The Wallaby is northeast of the Kangaroo and immediately adjacent to it.

265 NORTH LEDGE TRAVERSE
I, 5.6; protection unknown (not shown)

Begin by climbing to a small amphitheater on the Kangaroo's uphill (northeast) side. Climb a small chimney between it and the connecting formation called Joey, then move right and up on several ascending faults. Protection is very poor. The North Ledge offers unusual climbing; the rock, however, is the usual trash.

266 SOUTH FACE
I, 5.6-A1; protection unknown (not shown)

From the base of the southeast face of Joey, climb to the Kangaroo-Joey chimney. Climb south until a wide furrow is reached. Use several aid moves to reach the top.

267 JOEY—SOUTHWEST SIDE
I, 5.1; protection unknown (not shown)

Climb to a small amphitheater on the Kangaroo's uphill (northeast) side. Climb a small chimney above to a notch between the Kangaroo and Joey. Finish via a short stretch of shattered rock to the summit. Poorly protected and not recommended.

268 WALLABY
I, 5.9; bolt protection (not shown)

The route starts on the northeast ridge and climbs the face above.

Opossum, Tail, and Brogan Spire Complex
South Side

The south side of this formation is uphill from the Kangaroo.

269 WEST GULLY

I, 5.4; nuts to 1½" (not shown)

Walk uphill on the south side of the formation into an amphitheater that faces west. Within this amphitheater is a large cave with a sharp upper lip. *First Pitch:* Use a shoulder stand or boulder (5.10A or B) to reach the lip. Mantle over the lip and climb into a gully. Climb slabs to a col between Brogan Spire and the Tail. *Second Pitch:* Climb to the summit of Brogan Spire. Rappel.

270 *Variation*

5.7 (not shown)

The slabs on the first pitch can be gained by using a crack to the left of the cave.

271 CAVE ROUTE

I, 5.4; protection unknown (not shown)

Skirt the south end of a subsidiary buttress running down from the summit of Brogan. Walk along its east wall, passing through a cave along the way. Rope up at a vertical wall with huge buckets just past the cave. *First Pitch:* Climb the wall. *Second Pitch:* Pass through a unique hole and hike up to a col between the Tail and Brogan. *Third Pitch:* Climb to the summit of Brogan Spire. Rappel.

272 *Variation:* SOUTH BUTTRESS

5.4 (not shown)

The unique hole can be reached via the adjoining buttress mentioned at the start.

Miscellaneous Pinnacles

There is a fair amount of rock to the east of the Marsupial Crags. Little is known about this area except for the following 2 formations.

273 LOST HARDWARE PINNACLE

I, 5.6; protection unknown (not shown)

East and over the hill from the Wombat are several large pinnacles. The largest, Lost Hardware Pinnacle, has a route which begins on the west side. Traverse right to an exposed move on the southwest corner, then follow easy slabs to the top. Rappel.

274 TASMANIAN DEVILS

I, 5.1; protection unknown (not shown)

Near the top of a ridge ¾ mile northeast of the summit of Burma Road is an isolated tower. Climb a chimney on the south side of the tower. Walk off. Probably not worth the walk.

Mendenhall Ridge—Indian Ridge

The pinnacles north of Smith Rock overlook much of the Central Oregon area and are, for the first-time visitor, the most prominent formations. It is for this reason that most of the early recorded climbing took place there. More recently, the easy access afforded to early visitors along the North Unit Irrigation Canal Road has been closed to the public. A stiff 2 to 3 hour walk from Smith Rock State Park is currently required to reach the climbs. This, combined with the uniformly poor rock, will discourage all but the most die-hard Smith Rock aficionados.

Squaw Rock

Squaw Rock sits on the crest of a large east-west ridge, due north of Smith Rock. It is the largest pinnacle within the Mendenhall-Indian Ridge group, and the only spire visible when approaching from the north or south along U.S. 97.

275 SPIRAL

I, 5.1; protection unknown (not shown)

Climb to a ledge on the southeast side. Climb up and right, eventually reaching the west face. Scramble up a gully to the summit.

276 *Variation*

5.5 (not shown)

From a platform on the north side, jam a diagonal crack to an easy summit scramble.

277 SOUTH FACE
I, 5.2 (not shown)
Climb a series of ledges on the south side to the summit.

Leaning Brave

Leaning Brave is a 120' spire on the hillside southeast of Squaw Rock.

278 NORTH FACE
I, 5.7; protection unknown (not shown)
Start in a notch on the north side. Traverse right 10', then follow easy rock to the top. Rappel.

Papoose

A small pillar east of Squaw Rock and Leaning Brave.

279 SOUTHEAST RIDGE
I, 4 (not shown)
Climb the southeast ridge to the notch in the summit arete. Follow the arete to the top.

Poplar

North of Indian Ridge (which contains Squaw, Leaning Brave, and Poplar) is a second subsidiary ridge known as Mendenhall Ridge. Poplar is the most prominent tower on this ridge. Its overhanging poplar tree shape is clearly visible to the east from U.S. 97, near Crooked River Bridge.

280 SOUTH CHIMNEY
I, 5.7; protection unknown (not shown)
Climb the obvious chimney/crack system in the south face of the Poplar. Rappel. Two ropes are required.

Sapling

This is a small spire located several feet southwest of Poplar.

281 TILTED SLAB
I, 5.1; protection unknown (not shown)
Climb up the northeast face for 20' to a slab. From the slab, scramble up a ledge leading to the south face, then to the top.

Opposite, Mendenhall Ridge and Indian Ridge (Jeff Thomas photo)

5 STEIN'S PILLAR

Stein's Pillar has been included because of the wide exposure it has received in other guides, and because both routes can be done as free climbs. To reach the Pillar, follow U.S. 26 east from Prineville until close to the eastern end of Ochoco Reservoir. Turn left (north) and follow Mill Creek Road approximately 7 miles. Drive past the Pillar and park in a small turnout with a sign labeled "Stein's Pillar—Height 350 Feet." Cross the valley bottom and follow a trail which leads to the northeast face.

1 NORTHEAST FACE
III, 5.11A; nuts to 1¾"

Lots of weird protection and loose rock, but the climb is still enjoyable. The last pitch is probably one of the most entertaining in Oregon because it overhangs the entire lead and has relatively good rock. Except for a small detour on the third pitch, this route can be freed by following the original aid line. *First Pitch:* Stem a chimney just above a cave on the northeast side. Belay on a large ledge. *Second Pitch:* From the right side of the first ledge, climb a right-facing corner, then face climb up and left to a second ledge. *Third Pitch:* Move left and climb a short crack system, then face climb to a bulge. Traverse up and left on rotten holds until it is possible to traverse back right. Climb an overhang to a large split-level ledge halfway up the northeast face. *Fourth Pitch:* From the upper ledge, fight up and left past an overhang. Climb up and left to a large black knob and belay. *Fifth Pitch:* Strenuous face climbing leads to the top. Rappel the route using 2 ropes.

2 *Variation*
A4

Start left of the cave on the first pitch. Follow a rotten seam to the belay at the end of the second pitch on the regular route. Continue in the rotten aid crack until a difficult traverse permits you to rejoin the regular route at the third belay.

3 SOUTHWEST FACE
III, 5.10D; nuts to 1¾" (not shown)

A very good route, except for the 20' run-out on the second pitch and rotten rock on the crux. Start below an obvious dihedral system on the southwest face. *First Pitch:* Climb the dihedral to a bolt belay. *Second Pitch:* Traverse left 10' and face climb straight up past a bolt to an overhang. Move left under the overhang to its end. Belay at 4 bolts.

Stein's Pillar—Northeast Face (Jeff Thomas photo)

Third Pitch: Overcome a bulge above the belay and traverse back right. Buckets make a second overhang possible and lead to a crack. Climb "the final bulge" (crux) above and belay. **Fourth Pitch:** Move left up a slanting crack and easy face climbing to the summit. Rappel down the north side route using 2 ropes.

117

APPENDIX: CLIMBING HISTORY

Author's Note: This appendix lists first ascent data for all the climbs in this book. I have not been able to talk with every climber about every route, and I have on occasion probably misunderstood what was said. Any mistakes are sincerely regretted. Corrections and additions are welcome.

The following definitions will help interested readers interpret the first ascent data:

FA—First ascent

FFA—First free ascent

FRA—First recorded ascent; it is likely that the climb was done previously, but no record exists as to who did it.

FRFA—First recorded free ascent

Multiple attempts—After failing, the rope and protection were removed and the climber returned another day.

Tension—Weighting the protection system by grabbing or hanging on protection or by falling

Yo–yoing—Lead partners establishing successively higher top–ropes for each other.

Pre-placed Protection—Placing protection on rappel.

Top-roping—Climbing a route with a top rope before leading it.

Broughton Bluff Ascents

1 and 3 Gandalf's Grip and Variation II—FA via regular route 1968, Steve Strauch, John Haek; FFA via Variation II, Sept. 28, 1969, Steve Strauch, Jim O'Connell.

2 Variation I: Leaning Pillar—FA 1977, Bob McGown, Terry Yates.

4 Peach Cling—FA 1972, Jim Mayers, Gail Van Hoorn; FFA summer, 1978, Doug Bower and partner.

5 The Sickle—FRA after top-roping 1972, Ancil Nance.

6 Loose Block Overhang—FRA and probable FFA 1975, Monty Mayko, Jim Garrett.

7 Least Resistance—FRA 1971, Talbot Bielefeldt, Tim Carpenter, Bruce Weideman; FFA fall, 1975, Roger Baker.

8 Sandy's Direct—FA with pre-placed protection 1977, Bob McGown, Mike Smelsar, Sandy Regan.

9 Face Not Friction—FA 1975, Alan Campbell and partner; FFA after multiple attempts and pre-placed protection May 30, 1981, Mark Cartier.

10 Hanging Gardens—FA 1965, Bob Waring, John Wells, Bruce Holcomb; FRFA 1974, Rich Borich.

11 Variation I: BFD—FA 1975, Bruce Casey, Monty Mayko.

12 **Variation II: Mr. Potato**—FA 1972 or 1973, Alan Campbell and partner; FFA after multiple attempts July 18, 1981, Bruce Casey, Jeff Thomas.
13 **Variation III: Fun in the Mud**—FA 1977, Bob McGown, Terry Yates.
14 **Variation IV: Sesame Street**—FA 1972 Alan Campbell, Gail Van Hoorn; FFA July 8, 1973, Dean Fry and partner.
15 **Variation V: Demian**—FA with tension, fall 1976, Bob McGown, Mike Smelsar; FFA unknown.
16 **Variation VI: Endless Sleep**—FA spring, 1977, Bob McGown, Mike Smelsar.
17 **Variation VII: Peer Pressure**—FA 1972 or 1973, Jim Mayers, Alan Campbell; FFA with pre-placed protection spring, 1977, Mike Smelsar, Bob McGown.
18 **Variation VIII: Scorpion Seams**—FA 1980, Bob McGown, Steve Hillenger, Mike Corning.
19 **Classic Crack**—FA and FFA unknown; top-roped free in 1972 by Jim Mayers; led free in 1975 by Doug Bower after he top-roped it.
20 and 22 **Physical Graffiti and Variation II**—FA with tension via Variation II summer, 1977, Bob McGown, Mike Smelsar; FFA summer, 1977, Doug Bower and partner.
21 **Variation I: Hit the Highway**—FA after multiple attempts 1978, Bruce Casey, Monty Mayko.
23 **Red Eye**—FA first pitch 1976, Monty Mayko, Bruce Casey; FA complete climb with tension 1978, Mark Cartier and partner; FFA after multiple attempts Oct. 3, 1978, Jeff Thomas, Paul Gleeson.
24 **Critical Mass**—FA after multiple attempts summer, 1981, Bob McGown and partner.
25 **Sheer Stress**—FA 1976, Bruce Casey, Monty Mayko; FFA of the first 30', 1976, Ken Currens, Paul Landrum, Steve Strauch, Dan Foote; FFA of complete climb unknown.
26 **Variation**—FA June, 1981, Jay Kerr, Jim Olson.
27 **Journey to the Center of the Brain**—FA 1976, Mike Smelsar, Herb Olson.
28 **Walk on the Wild Side**—FA 1977, Jay Kerr, David Howe.
29 **Spidermonkey**—FA 1977, Bob McGown, Mark Simpson.
30 **Fruit Bat**—FA 1977, Bob McGown, Doug Bower.
31 **Variation**—FA 1977, Bob McGown, and partner.
32 **The Spring**—FA 1977, Bob McGown, Bruce Casey.
33 **Hanging Tree**—FA with pre-placed protection June 2, 1977, Bob McGown, Jeff Thomas.
34 **Unnamed aid route**—FA unknown.
35 **Snap, Crackle, Pop**—FA 1977, Bruce Casey, Monty Mayko.
36 **Superstition**—FA with tension 1977, Bob McGown, Scott Woolums; FFA July 11, 1981, Jeff Thomas, Mark Cartier.
37 **Well Hung**—FA 1977, Bob McGown, Mark Simpson; FFA unknown, but in April, 1977, Dan Foote and Bruce Casey yo-yoed the route.
38 **Variation: Mystic Void**—FA 1977, Bob McGown, Scott Woolums.
39 **Gold Arch**—FA 1978, Bob McGown, Doug Bower, Terry Yates.
40 **Shadow Dancing**—FA 1979, Bob McGown, Jim Olson, Mark Simpson.

Beacon Rock Ascents

1 **Obnoxious Cubby Hole**—FA 1977, Dick Morse, Chet Sutterlin.
2 **Southeast Face**—FA April 29, 1954, John Ohrenschall, Gene Todd.
3 **Variation I**—FA 1974, Steve Lyford and partner.
4 **Variation II: The Lost Variation**—FA May, 1958, Charlie Carpenter, Paul Resta.
5 **Right Gull**—FA 1965, Dean Caldwell, Chuck Erwin; FFA Oct. 1972, Dean Fry.
6 **Wrong Gull**—FA unknown; FFA Aug. 31, 1977, Jeff Thomas, Shari Kearney, Jack Holmgren.
7 **Seagull**—First pitch Sept. 3, 1977, Bob McGown, Jeff Thomas; complete climb Oct. 4, 1977, Jeff Thomas, Jim Dunavant.
8 **Left Gull**—FA 1965, Dean Caldwell, Chuck Erwin; FRFA July 6, 1973, Jeff Thomas, Steve Lyford.
9 **Bluebird**—FA 1972, Jeff Elphinston, Dave Mention; FFA Sept. 11, 1976, Jeff Thomas, Monty Mayko, Ed Newville.
10 **Variation I: Bluebird Direct**—FA Oct. 16, 1977, Jeff Thomas, Bruce Casey.
11 **Variation II: Sufficiently Breathless**—FA after top-roping summer, 1977, Scott Woolums, Terry Yates.
12 **Variation III**—FA original finish 1972, Jeff Elphinston, Dave Mention.
13 **Blownout**—FA Jan. 19–20, 1969, Steve Strauch, Danny Gates; FFA Oct. 16, 1976, after multiple attempts, Jeff Thomas, Ken Currens.
14 **Variation: Second Wind**—FA fall, 1981 after multiple attempts, Ted Johnson, Bill Strayer.
15 **The Grunge Book**—FA May, 1970, Wayne Haack, Steve Strauch.
16 **Wild Turkeys**—FA summer, 1970, Brian Holcomb, Neal Olson, Glen Kirkpatrick.
17 **Smooth Dancer**—FA summer, 1974, Alan Kearney, Les Nugent, Malcolm Ulrich.
18 **Dirty Double Overhang**—FA July, 1973, Alan Kearney, Dave Harry, Malcolm Ulrich.
19 **Take Fist**—FA with tension spring, 1981, Ted Johnson, Mike Pajanus; FFA June 29, 1981, Mark Cartier, Jeff Thomas.
20 **Diagonal Desperation**—FA with tension 1978, Bob McGown, Scott Woolums.
21 **Riverside**—FA Oct. 13, 1977, Jeff Thomas, Jim Dunavant.
22 **Flying Swallow**—FA 1965, Kim Schmitz, Earl Levin, Dean Caldwell; FFA April 27, 1977, Jeff Thomas, Del Young.
23 **Variation**—FA Aug. 10, 1977, Jeff Thomas, Mark Cartier.
24 **Flight Time**—FA with tension July, 1977, Jeff Thomas, Mark Cartier; FFA Aug. 1, 1981 after multiple attempts, Jeff Thomas, Mark Cartier.
25 **Flying Circus**—Lower pitch June 18, 1977, Jeff Thomas, Neal Olson; complete route June 22, 1977, Jeff Thomas, Mike Smelsar.
26 **Blood, Sweat, and Smears**—FA July 20, 1977, Jeff Thomas, Bob McGown.
27 **True Grunt**—FA July, 1977, Jeff Thomas, Mark Cartier.
28 **Steppenwolf**—FA May, 1971, Les Nugent, Bill Herman, Bill Nickle; first pitch free with upper half of True Grunt, May, 1977, Bob McGown, Levi Gray; second pitch free after traversing from Dod's

Jam June 12, 1977, Bob McGown, Mike Smelsar. Upper pitches with falls, tension and yo-yoing July 1978, Bob McGown, Doug Bower.

29 **Dod's Jam**—FA to Big Ledge, summer, 1961, Eugene Dod, Bob Martin, Earl Levin; FA to Grassy Ledges rappel, 1965, Kim Schmitz, Earl Levin; FA complete route May, 1972, Jeff Thomas, Dean Fry; FFA with tension, summer, 1972, Wayne Arrington, Jack Barrar.

30 **Variation I: Dod's Deviation**—FA June 12, 1977, Bob McGown, Mike Smelsar.

31 **Variation II: Dastardly Crack**—FA 1965, Bob Martin, Kim Schmitz, Eugene Dod, Gerald Bjorkman; FFA July 6, 1973, Jeff Thomas, Steve Lyford.

32 **Variation III: Squeeze Box**—FA July 20, 1977, Bob McGown, Jeff Thomas.

33 **Free for All**—FA August, 1973, Dean Fry, Steve Lyford.

34 **Free for Some**—FA unknown; an ascent with tension was made in summer, 1977, Bob McGown, Mike Smelsar; FFA unknown but Henry Barber may have done it in 1978.

35 **Pipeline**—FA with tension summer, 1977, Bob McGown; FFA Aug. 2, 1981 after multiple attempts, Ted Johnson, Charlie Priest.

36 **Updraft to Heaven**—FA with tension June, 1977, Bob McGown, Levi Gray.

37 **Jensen's Ridge**—FA 1968, Bob Martin, Dave Jensen; top-roped free July 28, 1973, Dean Fry; FFA April 13, 1974 after multiple attempts, Jeff Thomas.

38 **Variation: Mostly Air**—FA summer 1981, Bob McGown, Mark Simpson.

39 **Lay Lady Lay**—FA June 1977, Bob McGown, Doug Bower.

40 **Rip City**—FA July 9, 1977, Jeff Thomas, Mike Smelsar.

41 **Hard Times**—FA July 3, 1977, Jeff Thomas.

42 **Ragtime**—FA with tension Nov. 12, 1976, Jeff Thomas, Willis Krause; FFA 1981, Ted Johnson, Del Young.

43 **Boulder Problem in the Sky**—FA April 4, 1974, Jeff Thomas, Tim Miller; FFA Nov. 11, 1976 after many attempts, Jeff Thomas, Chet Sutterlin.

44 **Variation**—FA Oct. 22, 1976, Del Young, Jeff Thomas.

45 **On the Move**—FA with tension July 8, 1977, Bob McGown, Muriel Lodder.

Smith Rock Ascents

1 **Scorpio**—FA April, 1977, Curt Haire, Ray Stewart.

2 **Variation: I Lost My Lunch**—FA Oct. 19, 1980, Mark Cartier, Jim Anglin.

3 **Fool's Overture**—Mike Smelsar did the first several pitches with Ralph Moore. Mike returned fall, 1977 with Dana Horton to finish the climb.

4 **No Picnic**—FA July 3, 1981, Jim Anglin, Mike Hartley.

5 **Variation: Farmers' Variation**—FA fall 1981, Craig Benesch, Doug Kozlik.

6 and 7 Free Lunch and Unfinished Symphony—The original line of ascent was via Unfinished Symphony. The sequence went as follows: FA first two pitches of Unfinished Symphony summer, 1965, Kim Schmitz, Dean Caldwell; FA complete route via Unfinished Symphony April, 1972, Jeff Thomas, Steve Moore; FFA last two pitches via Unfinished Symphony May 6, 1972, Dean Fry, Larry Kemp; FA of Free Lunch with tension fall, 1976, Dan Foote, Mike Smelsar, Brian Holcomb; FFA complete route via Free Lunch Feb. 12, 1977, Jeff Thomas, Willis Krause; FFA 1982 after multiple attempts on first pitch of Unfinished Symphony, Alan Watts.

8 Soft Shoe Ballet—FA Nov., 1978, after multiple attempts, Bob McGown, Bill Antell, Jeff Alzner, Bruce Birchell.

9 Picnic Lunch Wall—FA Oct. 21–22, 1969, Kim Schmitz, Tom Bauman.

10 Journey to Ixtlan—FA bottom pitches March, 1979, Bob McGown, Jeff Alzner; FA top pitches by rappelling from the top to the previous high point summer, 1981, Bob McGown, Mark Simpson.

11 East Chimney—FA 1959, Jim and Jerry Ramsey.

12 West Gully—FA March, 1946, Ross Petrie, Dave Pearson.

13 City Dump—FA March 31, 1974, Steve Lyford, Jack Callahan, Jeff Thomas.

14 Vanishing Uncertainty—FA 1972, Andy Embick, Ted Schuck; FFA March 31, 1974, Jeff Thomas, Steve Lyford.

15 Waste Land—FA March 31, 1974, Jeff Thomas, Steve Lyford, Jack Callahan.

16 Shipwreck—FA Jan. 3, 1973, Dean Fry, Terri Raider.

17 and 18 Solar and Variation: No-Doz—FA via No-Doz Feb. 24, 1973, Dean Fry, Russ Bunker; FFA via Solar March 11, 1977, Jeff Thomas, Steve Strauch.

19 Cocaine Crack—FA with tension and yo-yoing July, 1979, Bob McGown, Doug Bower; FFA Nov. 13, 1981 after multiple attempts, Alan Watts, Kent Benesch.

20 Lion's Chair—FA Phil Dean led the first 2 pitches with Steve Hiem. He returned later in 1968 to finish the last 3 pitches with George Selfridge; FFA second and fourth pitches April 16–17, 1974, Bob McGown, Jeff Thomas; FFA complete climb May 6, 1977, after multiple attempts, Jeff Thomas, Ted Johnson.

21 Variation—FA 1968, Phil Dean, Steve Hiem.

22 and 23 Zebra and Variation I: Original Start—FA via Original Start 1970, Bob Martin, Ray Snyder; FA via potholes and tension, Jan. 14, 1973, Dean Fry, Jeff Thomas; FFA via potholes unknown; top-rope of Original Start free Aug. 29, 1981, after multiple attempts, Alan Watts.

24 Variation II: Zebra Direct—FA May 11, 1979, after multiple attempts, Alan Watts, Bill Ramsey.

25 Variation III: Zion—FA April 24, 1977, Jeff Thomas, Chris Mannix.

26 Lion's Jaw—FA 1960s, Tom and Bob Bauman.

27 Variation—FA unknown.

28 Pop Goes the Nubbin—FA Oct. 22, 1978, Jeff Thomas, Chris Jones.

29 Peanut Brittle—FA March 18, 1977, Jeff Thomas, Chet Sutterlin.

30 **Friday's Jinx**—FA unknown; FFA March 10, 1973, Dean and
Paul Fry.
31 **Variation I**—FA 1977 or 1978, Bill McKinney, Avary Tichner.
32 **Variation II**—FA 1977, Pat Carr and partner.
33 **Crack of Infinity**—FA second pitch April 7, 1974, Bob Grundy
and partner; FA second and third pitch 1976, Bob McGown, Mike
Smelsar; FA complete route March 19, 1977, Jeff Thomas, Chet
Sutterlin.
34 **Calamity Jam**—FA March 13, 1977, Jeff Thomas, Mike Smelsar.
35 and 36 **Pack Animal and Variation**—FA via Variation 1972,
Tom Rogers, Jeff Elphinston; FFA April 7, 1974, Jeff Thomas, Jack
Callahan; FFA via Variation March 18, 1977, Jeff Thomas, Chet
Sutterlin.
37 and 38 **Unnamed climbs**—FA unknown.
39 **Cinnamon Slab**—FA first pitch 1967, Alan Amos, George
Cummings; FA complete climb 1969, Wayne Haack, Phil Dean; this
climb was also free soloed by Bob Bauman but the date of ascent is
unknown.
40 **Variation: Cinnamon Toast**—FA March 19, 1977, Jeff Thomas, Chet
Sutterlin, Tim Carpenter, Roseann Lehman.
41 **Karate Crack to the Peapod**—Top-rope on first pitch, aid on second
pitch fall 1966, Dean Caldwell, Byron Babcock; FFA Nov. 7, 1973,
Dean Fry, Steve Lyford.
42 and 43 **Tator Tots and Variation: Karot Tots**—FA with pre-
placed protection via Karot Tots (formerly known as Euclid's
Column) Oct. 31, 1970, Dave Jensen, George Cummings; FFA via
regular route Feb. 26, 1977, Jeff Thomas, Mike Smelsar; FFA via
Karot Tots fall 1980, Alan Watts, Mark Cartier.
44 **Variation II**—FA via a fairly moderate line, summer, 1979,
by Alan Watts. Also via a very difficult way, summer, 1979, by Chris
Jones.
45 **Upper Ceiling**—FRA 1960s, Dean Caldwell, Jim Kindler.
46 **Variation**—FA Nov. 4, 1972, Jeff Thomas, Dean Fry.
47 **Sunshine Dihedral**—FA first pitch date unknown, Tom Bauman;
FA complete climb Feb. 13, 1971, Tom Rodgers, Dan Muir, Jack
Barrar; top-roped free July 6, 1979, Chris Jones, Alan Watts. FFA
after top-roping, pre-placed protection, and multiple attempts July 18,
1981, Alan Watts, Alan Lester.
48 **Moonshine Dihedral**—FA first pitch 1963, Dave Jensen, Bob Pierce;
FA unknown; FRFA Nov. 4, 1972, Dean Fry, Jeff Thomas.
49 **Rattlesnake Chimney**—FA May 1963, George Cummings, John
Hall.
50 **Bookworm**—FA unknown.
51 **Methuselah's Column**—FA last pitch March 10, 1973, Dean and
Paul Fry; FA first pitch March 26, 1977, Jeff Thomas, Ken Currens.
52 **Lycopodophyta**—FA Dec. 17, 1972, Dean Fry, Jeff Thomas.
53 **Deteriorata**—FA March 3, 1974, Jeff Thomas, Steve Lyford.
54 **Air to Spare**—FA Feb. 27–28, 1981, Jim Anglin, Tom Blust.
55 **Shoes of the Fisherman**—FA March 31, 1975, Jeff Thomas, Ralph
Moore; FFA April 24, 1977, after multiple attempts, Jeff Thomas.

56 **Wartley's Revenge**—FA 1972 Tom Rogers, Wayne Haack, Ken Jern; FFA Nov. 4, 1978, after multiple attempts, Jeff Thomas, Chris Jones.

57 **The Beard**—FRA Oct. 13, 1968, Tom Bauman, Jan Newman.

58 **Golgotha**—FA with pre-placed protection June 20, 1981, Alan Watts, Mel Johnson.

59 **Variation: Temptation**—FA March 17, 1981, Alan Watts, Wayne Kamara.

60 **New Testament**—FA unknown; FFA with tension Feb. 18, 1973, Dean Fry, Larry Kemp.

61 **Revelations**—FA with pre-placed protection 1975, Tim Carpenter, John Tyreman.

62 **Old Testament**—FA unknown.

63 **Heathens' Highway**—FA Oct. 28, 1979, Jim Anglin, Mike Hartley.

64 **Gothic Cathedral**—FA mid-1960s by either Bob Bauman and Ken Jern, or Dean Caldwell and John Darah.

65 **Variation I: Last Gasp**—FA 1972, Tom Rogers, Clay Cox.

66 **Variation II: Safety Valve**—FA Dec. 1967, Kim Schmitz, Eugene Dod.

67 **Charlie's Chimney**—FRA 1967, Dean Caldwell, Val Kiefer.

68 **Tinker Toy**—FA Feb. 19, 1978, Jeff Thomas, Alan Watts, Bill Ramsey.

69 **Bowling Alley**—FRA 1967, Dean Caldwell, Val Kiefer.

70 **Double Stain**—FA 1969, Dave Jensen.

71 **Toys in the Attic**—FA July 19, 1979, Bill Ramsey, Chris Jones.

72 **Variation: Child's Play**—FA July 5, 1980, Alan Watts, Bruce Birchell.

73 **Hesitation Blues**—FA Aug. 23, 1980, Alan Watts, Kent Benesch, after top-roping.

74 **Toy Blocks**—FA May 28, 1977, Jeff Thomas, Shari Kearney.

75 **Variation: Self-Preservation Variation**—FA Aug. 25, 1979, Mike Hartley, Jim Anglin.

76 **Dancer**—FA first pitch with pre-placed protection 1976, Tim Carpenter, John Tyreman. FA complete climb Feb. 14, 1976, Jeff Thomas, Ken Stroud.

77 **The Asterisk**—FRA 1961, Jim and Jerry Ramsey.

78 **Skyways**—FA with tension May 11, 1974, Jeff Thomas, Doug Phillips, Scott Hansen. FFA fall 1981, Mark Cartier, Jim Anglin.

79 **Sky Chimney**—FA with tension fall 1969, Dave Jensen, George Cummings; FFA winter, 1974, Doug Phillips, Jack Callahan.

80 **Variation: Byways**—FRA July 4, 1980, Jean Yves Poublan, Walt Algar.

81 **White Satin**—FA March 11, 1974, Jeff Thomas, Doug Phillips.

82 **Black Velcro**—FA first 3 pitches 1975, Bob Johnson, Doug Phillips; FA complete route Aug. 19, 1978, Jeff Thomas, Mark Cartier.

83 **Snibble Tower**—FA 1969, Jon Marshall, John Haek; FFA 1976, Alan and Shari Kearney.

84 **Smith Summit—East Wall and East Summit**—FA May 27, 1973, Dean Fry, Wayne Arrington; FFA Feb. 23, 1974, Jeff Thomas, Steve Lyford.

85 **Carabid**—FA 1977, Chet Sutterlin, Bob Bury.

86 **Phoenix**—FA winter 1976, Ken Currens.
87 **Kunza Korner**—FA 1976 or 1977, Ralph Moore and partner. FFA June 9, 1980 after multiple attempts, Alan Watts.
88 **Cod Rock**—**Sunset Boulevard**—FA 1972, Bob Marshall, Wayne Haack.
89 **Culls in Space**—FA June 3, 1980, Jim Anglin, Mike Hartley.
90 **Arrowpoint**—FA unknown.
91 **Shaft**—FA 1974, Steve Lyford and partner.
92 **Platform**—**South Arete**—FRA 1960, Jim Ramsey, Jack Watts.
93 **Smith Summit**—**West Summit**—FA June 1967, Charles Dotter, Tony Bates, Jeff Dotter, Marcia Bilbao.
94 **No Brain, No Pain**—FA with tension July 19, 1979, Jeff Thomas, Bill Ramsey; FFA after top-roping April 25, 1981, Alan Watts, Alan Lester.
95 **Variation I: No Pain, No Gain**—FA summer 1981, Alan Watts; FFA with pre-placed protection Aug. 17, 1981, Alan Watts, Alan Lester.
96 **Variation II**—FA summer 1981, Alan Watts, Bill Ramsey.
97 **Tears of Rage**—FA summer, 1981 after multiple attempts, Alan Watts, Alan Lester.
98 **Bits and Pieces**—FA April, 1977, Brian Holcomb, Dan Foote, Don Johnson.
99 **Skylight**—FA July, 1979, Jeff Thomas, Chris Jones; FFA July 18, 1979 after multiple attempts, Jeff Thomas, Bill Ramsey.
100 and 102 **Sky Ridge and Variation II: Skydiver**—FA via Skydiver after pre-placing protection 1968, Dave Jensen, George Cummings; FA via regular route 1973, Steve Lyford, Scott Schmitt; FFA via Skydiver winter, 1981, Tom Blust, Spurge Cochran.
101 **Variation I**—FA August, 1972, Jeff Thomas, Tim Carpenter, Ed Beacham.
103 **The Awl**—**Inside Corner**—FA 1961, Jim and Jerry Ramsey; FFA with pre-placed protection Aug., 1961, Jim Ramsey, Bruce Hahn.
104 **Christian Brothers Traverse**—FA the Priest 1964, Kim Schmitz, Eugene Dod, Alan Amos; FA the Monk 1965, Bill Cummins, Jan Cummins, Ted Davis, Ken Wallen; FA the Friar 1964, Ted Davis, Jan Cummins; FA the Friar via Priest and Monk 1965, Ted Davis, Bill Cummins, Juli Beall; FFA the Friar 1964, Kim Schmitz; FA the Abbot 1964, Jon Marshall, Gerald Bjorkman.
105 **Fallen Angel**—FA after top-roping and pre-placed protection Oct. 1978, Mike Smelsar, Nancy Baker.
106 **Midriff Bulge**—FA Feb. 26, 1977, Jeff Thomas, Mike Smelsar.
107 **Snake**—FRA May 26, 1974, Jeff Thomas, Tim Carpenter.
108 **Variations I and II**—FA unknown.
109 **The Golden Road**—FA after multiple attempts and with pre-placed protection Aug. 1981, Kent Benesch, Tom Blust.
110 **Cling-On**—FA July 7, 1974, Jeff Thomas, Doug Phillips, Grote Phillips.
111 **Strung-Out**—FA July 7, 1974, Jeff Thomas, Doug Phillips, Grote Phillips.

112 **Angel Flight Buttress**—FA Oct. 1978, Mike Smelsar, Dick Morse.
113 **Heaven Can Wait**—FA Aug. 1979, Kent Benesch, Chris Haunold.
114 **High Sage**—FA Oct. 1978, Mike Smelsar, Mark Cartier.
115 **Tarantula**—FA with pre-placed protection and multiple attempts July 12, 1981, Alan Watts.
116 **Spiderman**—FA 1969, Steve Strauch, Danny Gates.
117 **Widow Maker**—FA spring, 1976, when Ken Currens climbed past the lieback with Dan Foote but backed off because of rotten rock. Dan returned and finished the pitch with a partner.
118 **Explosive Energy Child**—FA with pre-placed protection and tension fall 1976, Mike Smelsar, Bob McGown; FFA with pre-placed protection spring 1977, Mike Smelsar, John Tyreman.
119 **In Harm's Way**—FA Sept. 1975, Bob Johnson, Doug Phillips.
120 **Little Feat**—FA after multiple attempts June 16, 1980, Mike Hartley, Jim Anglin.
121 **Dr. Doom**—FA April 20, 1974, Jeff Thomas, Steve Lyford, Tim Miller, Tom Minderhout.
122 **Necromancer**—FA unknown.
123 **Captain Fingers**—FA fall 1980, Craig Benesch, Kent Benesch.
124 **Western Chimneys**—FA April 1963, George Cummings, Roger Peyton.
125 **Palo Verde**—FA Jan. 1, 1981, Mike Hartley, Jim Anglin.
126 and 127 **Unnamed cracks**—FA unknown.
128 **Chimney De Chelly**—FA March 25, 1977, Jeff Thomas, Ken Currens.
129 **Variation: Desolation Row**—FA June, 1981, Alan Watts, Tom Blust; FFA June 27, 1981, after multiple attempts, Alan Watts, Pat Carr.
130 **Tale of Two S#@%&**—FA first 2 pitches Dec. 4, 1977, Monty Mayko, Bruce Casey; FFA and first ascent of complete route Sept. 30, 1978, Jeff Thomas, Chris Jones, Mike Hartley.
131 **Down Syndrome**—FA first pitch Nov. 1978, Al and Shari Kearney; FA complete route top-roped and pre-placed protection winter, 1980, Chuck Buzzard.
132 **Minas Morgul**—FA 1972, Wayne Arrington; FFA May 3, 1981, with pre-placed protection and multiple attempts, Alan Watts.
133 **Variation**—FA with pre-placed protection fall, 1977, Avary Tichner.
134 **Trezlar**—FA 1972, Tom Rogers, Clay Cox, Bob Johnson; FFA April 3, 1976, Jeff Thomas, Jim Davis.
135 **Lichens Persuasion**—FA fall, 1978, Jon Sprecher, Pat Carr.
136 **Diamonds and Rust**—FA winter, 1979, Mark Cartier, Mike Smelsar.
137 **Perpetual Motion**—FA Mike Hartley, John Rich.
138 **Dolf's Dihedral**—FA spring, 1980, Bill Ramsey, Mary Ellen Dolf.
139 and 140 **Potential Energy and Variation**—FA via Variation fall, 1980, Alan Lester, Chuck Wheeler; FFA July 28, 1981, Alan Watts, John Barbella.
141 **King Kong**—FA 1967, Scott Arighi, Jim Nieland; FFA 1969 or 1970, Steve Strauch, Danny Gates.

142 **Variation I**—FA after top-roping and pre-placed protection July 27, 1978, Alan Watts, Bill Ramsey.

143 **Variation II**—FA unknown.

144 **Godzilla**—FRA 1969 or 1970, Steve Strauch, Danny Gates.

145 **Smaug**—FA second pitch 1970, Tom Rogers, Al Balmforth; FA complete climb Sept. 2, 1978, Jeff Thomas, Avary Tichner.

146 **Monkey Farce**—FA April 2, 1977, Jeff Thomas, Mike Smelsar.

147 **West Face Variation**—FA Sept. 11, 1965, Tom Bauman, Bob Ashworth; FFA April 9, 1967, Tom Bauman, Bob Ashworth.

148 **Variation I**—FA unknown.

149 **Variation II**—FA unknown.

150 **Southwest Corner**—FA 1970, Tom Bauman; FFA second pitch 1972 or 1973, Mike Seely; FFA third and fourth pitches April 3, 1977 after multiple attempts, Jeff Thomas, Mike Smelsar; FFA first pitch spring, 1980 after multiple attempts, Alan Watts.

151 and 152 **Variation I and Variation II**—FA unknown.

153 **Variation II**—FFA July 27, 1981, Alan Watts, John Barbella.

154 **West Face**—FA 1962, Dean Caldwell, Byron Babcock, Bill Lentsch.

155 and 156 **Northwest Passage and Variation**—FA second and third pitch via Variation, 1968, Tom Bauman, Bob Ashworth; FA complete route April 28, 1973, Jeff Thomas, Steve Moore; FFA first pitch (except bottom 4 bolts) July 26, 1981 after multiple attempts, Alan Watts; FFA second pitch Nov. 3, 1981, after multiple attempts, Alan Watts.

157 **North Face**—FA Dec., 1967, Dean Caldwell, Jim Kindler.

158 **East Face**—FA summer, 1964, Kim Schmitz, Gerald Bjorkman.

159 **Rising Expectations**—FA unknown; FFA Sept. 13, 1979 after multiple attempts, Chris Jones, Alan Watts.

160 **Pioneer Route**—FA Jan. 1, 1960, Dave Bohn, Jim Fraser, Vivian Staender.

161 **Bohn Street West Face Cave**—FA Jan. 1963, Dave Jensen, Bob Martin.

162 **Monkey Space**—FA 1978, Bob McGown and partner; FFA April 21, 1979 after multiple attempts, Chris Jones, Bill Ramsey.

163 **The Madcap Adventures of Mr. Toad**—FA Aug., 1978, Mike Smelsar, Tom Easthope.

164 **Chicken Little**—FA Aug., 1978, Mike Smelsar, Tom Easthope.

165 **Great Expectations**—FA March 6, 1977, Paul Fry, Jeff Thomas.

166 **Scabbies**—FA 1978, Mike Smelsar, John Tyreman.

167 **New World**—FA March, 1979, Mike Smelsar, Nancy Baker.

168 **Hawkline Monster**—FA 1980, Chuck Buzzard, solo.

169 **Bill's Flake**—FA Aug. 17, 1978, Bill Ramsey, Alan Watts.

170 **Paper Tiger**—FA of third and fourth pitches Aug. 27, 1978, Jeff Thomas, Mark Cartier; FA complete route Dec. 15, 1979, Mike Hartley, Jim Anglin.

171 **Super Slab**—FA 1969, Danny Gates; FFA 1970 or 1971, Danny Gates, Neal Olson.

172 **Variation I: Panama Express**—FA Jan. 2, 1980, Jim Anglin, Mike Hartley.

173 **Variation II: Panama Red**—FA 1979, Mike Smelsar, Mark Cartier.
174 **Variation III: Amphetamine Grip**—FA 1970, Danny Gates, Steve Strauch.
175 **Iron Curtain**—FA April 24, 1977, Jeff Thomas, Chris Mannix.
176 and 177 **Helter Skelter and Variation I**—FA first pitch May 8, 1977, Jeff Thomas, John Rakovsky; FA complete climb via Variation spring 1978, Mike Smelsar, Ed Newville.
178 **Variation II: If Six Were Nine**—FA June 1979, Bruce Birchell and partner.
179 **Chairman Mao's Little Red Book**—FA unknown; FFA July 21, 1979, Jeff Thomas, Chris Jones, Alan Watts.
180 **Fingers of Fate**—FA June 30, 1979, Mike Hartley, Jim Anglin; FFA fall, 1979 after multiple attempts, Alan Lester.
181 **Gone with the Flake**—FA Dec. 15, 1974, Jeff Thomas, Roger Robinson.
182 **Ho Chi Minh Trail**—FA 1969, Wayne Haack, Steve Strauch.
183 **Shanghai**—FA July 17, 1978, Bill Ramsey, Alan Watts.
184 **Peking**—FA May 5, 1969, Tom Bauman, Osa Thatcher.
185 **Moscow**—FA 1965, Pat Callis, Mickey Schurr.
186 **Variation: Mongolians**—FA Oct. 1, 1978, Chris Jones, Jeff Thomas.
187 **Havana**—FA unknown.
188 **I Almost Died**—FA Aug. 1978, Avary Tichner; FFA Oct. 28, 1978 after multiple attempts, Jeff Thomas, Ken Currens.
189 **Red Ryder**—FA 1975, Wayne Haack, Steve Thompson.
190 **Variation: Flex**—FA unknown.
191 **The Young and the Restless**—FA with pre-placed protection Sept. 1976, Dan Foote, Mike Smelsar.
192 **Variation: The Young and the Worthless**—FA summer, 1979, Cheri Richardson, Alan Lester.
193 **London Tower**—FA April 14, 1973, Dean Fry, Russ Bunker and a third partner.
194 **Chockstone Chimney**—FA 1959, Jim and Jerry Ramsey.
195 **Victory of Proletarian People's Ambition Arete**—FA spring, 1980, Brian Holcomb, Steve Martin.
196 **North Ridge**—FA unknown.
197 **Abraxas**—FA lower pitches 1969, Steve Strauch, Wayne Haack; FA complete route 1969, Steve Strauch, Danny Gates; FFA fifth pitch 1977, Wayne Arrington, Ken Currens; FFA second and third pitches, 1981, Mark Cartier, Mark Jonas.
198 **Sands of Time**—FA fall, 1977, Todd Rentchler.
199 **Southeast Face**—FA June, 1966, Ted Davis, Willy Zeigler.
200 **Osa Thatcher's Needle**—FA unknown.
201 **Bird Dung Chimney**—FA unknown.
202 **Deception Crack**—FA 1970, Bruce Burling, Frank Jager; FFA June 4, 1977, Jeff Thomas, Ted Johnson.
203 **Street Walker**—FA Dec. 7, 1974, Jeff Thomas, Cindy Jones.
204 **Brain Salad Surgery**—FA March 28, 1976 after multiple attempts, Jeff Thomas.
205 **Juniper Gully**—FA 1960, Dean Caldwell, Byron Babcock.
206 **North Side**—FA 1954, Jack Janacek, J. Harrower.

207 **The Ear**—FA 1969, Tom Rogers and party.
208 **Unnamed aid climb**—FA March 24, 1969, Tom Bauman, Bob Ashworth.
209 **Jamboree**—FA unknown.
210 **Rib Traverse**—FA unknown.
211 **Instant Replay**—FRA 1969, Tom Rogers, Steve Wilson.
212 **Parking Lot Crack**—FRA mid-1960s, Bob Bauman, free solo.
213 **Out-of-Control**—FA with tension May 14, 1977, Jeff Thomas, Mike Smelsar; FFA unknown.
214 **Midnight Rider**—FA 1955, Viv and Gil Staender; FRFA May 14, 1977, Jeff Thomas, Mike Smelsar.
215 **Free Spirit**—FRA April 28, 1974, Jeff Thomas, Scott Hansen.
216 **D.A.R. Crack**—FA 1970, Tom Rogers, John Sanborn, Don Johnson; FFA April 28, 1974, Jeff Thomas, Scott Hansen.
217 **North Side**—FRA 1954, Don Comer, Dick Pooley, Dave Hitchcock.
218 **Slopper**—FA winter, 1981, Craig Benesch, Doug Kozlik.
219 **Chopper**—FA summer, 1971, Del Young, Dave Jensen.
220 **Sunjammer**—FA after top-roping summer, 1971, Del Young, Mead Hargis.
221 **Thrasher**—FA April 28, 1974, Jeff Thomas, Scott Hansen.
222 **Easy Street**—FA unknown.
223 **Juniper Snag**—FRA 1961, Jim Ramsey, Clinton DeShazer.
224 **Limestone Chimney**—FRA 1955, Viv and Gil Staender.
225 **Bump and Grind**—FA 1969, Ray Smutek, Iain Lynn; FFA unknown.
226 **Lost Fox**—FA 1973, Steve Lyford and partner.
227 **Skid Row**—FA Nov. 3, 1974, Jeff Thomas, Charley Brown.
228 **East Chimney**—FRA 1963, Bruce Hahn, Jim Ramsey.
229 **South Buttress**—FRA 1956, Viv and Gil Staender.
230 **Lower West Chimney**—FRA 1956, Viv and Gil Staender.
231 **Lieback Flake**—FRA 1970, Miles and Dorothy Paul.
232 **Direct Northwest Crack**—1958, Jim and Jerry Ramsey.
233 **Deliverance**—FA with a top rope only, 1970, Tom Rogers.
234 **Smut**—FRA 1960, Dave Jensen and partner; FFA Jan. 4, 1981 after multiple attempts, Alan Watts.
235 **Falling Rock Zone**—FA unknown.
236 **Northwest Corner**—FRA 1961, Jim Ramsey, Clinton DeShazer.
237 **Desiderata**—FA unknown; FFA March 6, 1974, Jeff Thomas, Jim Eliot.
238 **Defecation Crack**—FA unknown.
239 **Peanuts**—FA unknown.
240 **South Bowl**—FRA 1964, Jim Ramsey, Ken Bierly.
241 **North Ledge**—FA unknown.
242 **Rotten Crack**—FA 1956, Viv and Gil Staender; FFA date unknown, Kim Schmitz.
243 **Friction Arete**—FA 1965, Jim Rixon, Kim Schmitz.
244 **Orange Peel**—FA unknown.
245 **Lemon Peel**—FA unknown.
246 **Cow Pie**—FA unknown.
247 **Thin Air**—FA unknown; FFA Nov. 1972, Jeff Thomas, Steve Moore.
248 **Catty Corner**—FA 1974, Doug Phillips, Bob Johnson.

249 **Crazies**—FA 1972, Ed Beacham and partner; FFA unknown.
250 **Desert Solitaire**—FA Nov. 25, 1972, Jeff Thomas, Keith Edwards, Dean Fry.
251 **Round River**—FA unknown.
252 **Variation**—FA Oct. 26, 1974, Jeff Thomas.
253 **Catfight Cracks**—FA first pitch 1969 or 1970, Tom Rogers, Jack Barrar; FA complete climb Sept. 30, 1972, Dean Fry, Jeff Thomas.
254 **C.L. Concerto**—FA Sept. 13–14, 1972, Dean Fry, Jack Barrar.
255 **Green Gully**—FA Sept. 1967, Jon Marshall, Carol Anderson.
256 **Whitecloud**—FA April 10, 1971, Tom Rogers, Jack Barrar.
257 **The Thumb**—FA 1965, Ted Davis and party.
258 **Diagonal Crack**—FA 1960, Jim and Jerry Ramsey.
259 **Dogfight Crack**—FA Nov. 16, 1974, Jeff Thomas, Doug Phillips.
260 **Tail**—FA 1963, Ted Davis, Don Chattin.
261 **The Great Roof**—FA 1969, Wayne Haack, Jim Nieland.
262 **Pin Bender**—FA Feb. 17, 1973, Dean Fry, Russ Bunker.
263 **Mini Half Dome**—FA unknown.
264 **Delirium Tremens**—FRA 1970, Dave Jensen; FFA 1972 by either Del Young or Wayne Arrington.
265 **North Ledge Traverse**—FA 1963, Kim Schmitz, Alan Amos, Jon Marshall.
266 **South Face**—FA 1964, Eugene Dod, Gerald Bjorkman.
267 **Joey—Southwest Side**—FA 1961, Jim and Jerry Ramsey.
268 **Wallaby**—FA 1963, Kim Schmitz, Gerald Bjorkman; FFA Jan. 30, 1982, Alan Lester, Alan Watts.
269 **West Gully**—FA 1963, Ted Davis, Jon Marshall.
270 **Variation**—FA Nov. 2, 1974, Jeff Thomas, Guy Keene.
271 **Cave Route**—FA 1963, Ted Davis, Jon Marshall.
272 **Variation: South Buttress**—FRA 1970, Bruce and Brian Watson, Charles Cunningham.
273 **Lost Hardware Pinnacle**—FA unknown; FFA 1970, Tom Rogers, Jack Barrar, M. Youngblood, John Sanborn.
274 **Tasmanian Devils**—FA unknown.
275 **Spiral**—FRA 1956, Jim and Jerry Ramsey.
276 **Variation**—FRA 1963, Bruce Hahn, Jim Ramsey.
277 **South Face**—FRA 1957, John Ohrenschall, C. Richards.
278 **North Face**—FA 1963, Dave Jensen, Jim Benham.
279 **Southeast Ridge**—FRA 1963, Bruce Hahn, Jim Ramsey.
280 **South Chimney**—FA March, 1949, Ross Petrie, Dave Wagstaff, Bill Van Atta.
281 **Tilted Slab**—FA 1955, E.J. Zimmerman and party.

Stein's Pillar Ascents

1 **Northeast Face**—FA July, 1950, Floyd Richardson, Glenn Richardson, Don Baars, Leonard Rice, Rodney Shay; a nearly free ascent with tension and yo-yoing July 11, 1977, Bob McGown, Doug Bower; FFA July 12, 1979 after multiple attempts, Jeff Thomas, Bill Ramsey, Alan Watts.
2 **Variation**—FA July 28, 1965, Kim Schmitz, Dean Caldwell.
3 **Southwest Face**—FA Oct. 31, 1967, Jim Nieland, Eugene Dod; FFA July 23, 1977, Bob McGown, Jeff Thomas.

INDEX

Author Jeff Thomas (Phil Jones photo)

About the author:

Portland resident Jeff Thomas has been climbing mountains for more than a dozen years, including making first-ascents on Alaska's Mt. Hunter, Mt. Huntington and Dark Tower. In addition to extensive rock climbing experience throughout the United States and Canada, he's enjoyed many of the classic routes in Chamonix, France. In researching his first book, **Climbing Guide to Beacon Rock, Smith Rock and Stein's Pillar,** as well as this one, Thomas personally did more than 70% of the individual routes covered in **Oregon Rock**.

After receiving a bachelor's degree in resource recreation from Oregon State University, Thomas was a technical writer for both the Corps of Engineers and the U.S. Fish and Wildlife Service before opening his own tree service in Portland. He is a member of the American Alpine Club and past chairman of the Oregon Section of that organization.